Reflections on Being the CEO

Sir Steve Lancashire

A Forum Strategy Resource published by Cadogan Press

CADOGAN
PRESS

First Published 2023
Cadogan Press

© **2023 Forum Education Limited**

ISBN: 978-1-8380073-5-5

Set and designed by Cadogan Press
Printed by Book Printing UK

DEDICATION

In memory of my parents June and Terry Lancashire,
the rocks on which all waves crashed.

ABOUT THE AUTHOR

Sir Steve Lancashire is an accomplished Chief Executive, leadership thinker, and educationalist. He was the founder and CEO of REAch2, which was the largest primary academy trust in England, from 2012 until 2022, and has been involved in primary education for over thirty years.

He was previously a Headteacher and Executive Headteacher specialising in schools in challenging contexts. He has been a National Leader of Education and a lead adviser for the Department for Education. His international work includes working with school principals in Afghanistan, UAE, Singapore and Australia.

Today Sir Steve is Chair of Forum Strategy's National #TrustLeaders CEO network & a Forum Strategy Associate, offering mentoring to academy trust CEOs and working alongside Michael Pain on delivery of the *Being the CEO* programme. He also works with the Teacher Development Trust on executive leadership programmes and is a member of the advisory group at leading executive recruitment organisation Satis Education.

Steve was Knighted for services to education in the Queen's New Year's Honours list in 2016 and has been a driving force at the centre of many important groups and discussions around system leadership and improvement.

Contents

Foreword

When Sir Steve Lancashire became Chief Executive of REAch2 Academy Trust, well over a decade ago now, he commenced in a role for which no handbook had yet been written, at least in the schools sector. The first generation of academy trust Chief Executives were all taking a great leap into the darkness, recognising the huge potential of creating large scale, collaborative, and more autonomous education organisations led by accomplished educationalists; but at the same time knowing full well that they were first to do so. They were all pioneers, working out what their jobs, and their organisations, would look like. As with all pioneering sorts, while some of this breed overcame the obstacles and pitfalls to tell a tale of success and progress, others, sadly, failed along the way. Sir Steve made it out the other side, and with flying colours!

Driven - for the most part - by a desire to make a difference to more pupils and staff, this first generation of academy trust Chief Executives embarked upon this untrodden path with enormous enthusiasm and, for some, a spectacular disregard for the risks involved. Indeed, Sir Steve, in these pages, acknowledges his own eagerness to take some big risks, though his timely approach to generating good governance, risk management, and sustainable growth, helped set both him and his successful contemporaries apart. The stories and examples told so vividly in this book are a demonstration of that approach.

Indeed, when undertaking the research and writing of my book, *Being The CEO*, a few years back, I came to a firm conclusion: it is those Chief Executives that have an openness to learning, a deep well of curiosity, all of which is built upon a healthy degree of humility, that go on to generate the tools and genuine self-confidence to thrive in the role. Whilst some of Sir Steve's peers believed their career success as headteachers and executive headteachers meant they were already equipped with the answers to succeed in the CEO role (they didn't, far too many failed spectacularly in the job), others like Sir Steve, ramped their learning (and their professional relationships) up a notch.

In the collection of essays that make up this book, Sir Steve's journey of learning, openness to ideas, and his sense of curiosity in the job shines through. It is clear that relationships and partnerships - investing time and energy in aligning oneself and building connections with people who can, and are willing to help, and who share some important fundamental values - has been essential. That has meant looking across organisations, sectors, industries, and even countries to discover what it truly means both to involve others in supporting his and the organisation's work, and to keep striving to understand what it means to be a high-performing Chief Executive in an evolving context. It's also evident to me that while Sir Steve has demonstrated humility, he certainly did not disregard risk-taking altogether! As he so often says, the journey of a founder CEO has involved *'being willing to build the plane while we were flying it'*. It's just that it involved making sure he had the right crew onboard with him.

And let's be under no doubt, every CEO needs a little bit of luck. A strong Chair of trustees, a government willing to provide adequate funding and support, and an exceptionally strong appointment here and there (Sir Steve's Deputy CEO and Chief Operating Officer feature throughout) all matters. But we also, to some degree, make our own luck in the CEO role, and Sir Steve thought hard and worked hard on making a success of the role, and fostering the key relationships that underpinned both his and the organisation's success.

I am particularly honoured that Sir Steve has chosen to base his writings and his thinking loosely around my book and framework for *'Being The CEO'*. Our professional partnership goes back to the early days of his work establishing REAch2 Academy Trust and our collaboration in shaping that organisation's growth and direction, and Steve was a critical friend in helping me to solidify some of my ideas around what it means to be a thriving Chief Executive for the long-term. The chapters pick up on the six dimensions of organisational development as set out in *Being The CEO*[1], and provide some rich reflections, stories and questions that help to bring that framework even further to life.

---

[1] Being The CEO; the six dimensions of organisational leadership. Pain, 2019 John Catt Educational.

Indeed, on the topic of books about CEOs, a key publication on the CEO role - and one I would thoroughly recommend to those looking for inspiration across sectors - is that of William N. Thorndike Jr., and it's called 'The Outsiders'[2]. In analysing the work of the most successful Chief Executives of the second half of the twentieth century in the US, based on long-term metrics of success and performance, Thorndike notes a number of things. Amongst these are that they were almost all, like Sir Steve, first time CEOs. Few of them had undertaken MBAs but had a zest for learning on the job and from others, they made time for their loved ones and personal lives and interests, they believed in nimble central teams and operational support being as close to the frontline as possible, and they shirked many of the conventions of their sectors, looking outwards for so many of their ideas and much of their inspiration. Sir Steve's journey reflects so many of these characteristics.

What made the context for Sir Steve slightly different, and why so much learning exists in these pages for CEOs operating both within education and elsewhere, is that, until this point, the role of CEO had not existed before in the schools sector. Sir Steve, together with a small group of contemporaries worked it out again from scratch, and they learnt an enormous amount along the way. There was a blank canvas that provided all of us with an interest in the job - in whatever sector - with a unique opportunity to understand it yet again, from its very first principles. Steve's take on it, from so many angles, makes for a thoroughly interesting read.

The chapters of this book brim with honesty, humility, humour, ambition, integrity, and deep-rooted values. There are mistakes and there are great successes. It does not hold back in its vulnerability or its wisdom. But most of all, there are the rich and authentic stories of what it really means and feels like to be a successful, and human, Chief Executive over the course of a decade of change, uncertainty and uncharted territory. I hope you enjoy it as much as I did.

Michael Pain
Southwell, May 2023

---

[2] *Thorndike, William. The Outsiders: Eight Unconventional CEOs and Their Radically Rational Blueprint for Success. Boston, Mass; Harvard Business Review Press, 2012*

Introduction

Let's start at the very beginning

'Full many a flower is born to blush unseen and waste its sweetness on the desert air.'

There is something profoundly beautiful and yet achingly sad about the imagery contained within, what I think, is one of the greatest lines in English poetry and indeed one of the greatest English elegiac poems. I suspect for many of us of a certain age, Grey's 'Elegy written in a Country Churchyard' is very familiar. It was a staple part of any schooling in English literature during the 1970 and 1980s and as such, subject to much scrutiny and discourse. There are so many themes contained within the elegy, and I remember good-humoured debate about what it is *about*. For some, it is death as the great leveller of social class, for others it is an idealistic idyll to country life, part of it is clearly the poet reflecting on how he himself will be remembered and what posterity will make of him. To me though, it is primarily about two themes that resonated strongly with me then and have continued to do so throughout the whole of my personal and professional life.

The tragedy of unfulfilled potential and the injustice of opportunity denied.

I have this image in my mind of a single yellow crocus, glorious in its simplicity and overpowering in its fragrance blooming unnoticed and unappreciated in a scorching desert wasteland, eventually wilting and fading away. All its qualities lost. Romanticised I know, but if poetry is supposed to leave an impression, this certainly did on me.

The poem was revised twice and eventually published in 1751 and Grey took his muse from the gravestones in a churchyard in Stokes Poges. In observing these gravestones, he reflects on the lives of those buried there and, as well as all the other themes, he observes that among the deceased villagers are some who had the potential to be brilliant or powerful but were denied those things either by accident of birth or poverty or other factors out of their control. Ordinary working-class folk, probably living happy lives, yet unaware of what the wider world has to offer and limited or no opportunity to be socially mobile even with the undoubted talents many would have had. More palatable when it is a brilliant analogy using flowers and deserts, less so when you remember it is real people, and real lives.

I think it resonates so strongly with me because of the universal truths that sit within its messages, truths that are as relevant today, 270 years later, as they were then and truths that were relevant fifty years ago, when I was growing up.

I can't really imagine what it was like to be a working-class labourer in the fields all that time ago, but I do know what it was like to be a working-class boy fifty years ago, growing up in a mining community in Sheffield.

My dad was at first a joiner and then, in search of a more secure job, became a miner who, with all the overtime, seemed to work endless hours. My mum worked firstly in the local tool factory, then in the local food shop and latterly as a school dinner lady. My parents gave me and my two sisters a fantastic early childhood. Both, as do most parents, wanted the very best for us and ensured that we wanted for nothing. Like most families in mining communities the highlight of our year was a week's holiday in a caravan, our favourite places being Flamborough and Bridlington and at weekends our parents took us places or encouraged our sport and in the evenings they went to socialise at the miner's welfare club or ventured off into town to the bingo and we, like all kids on our estate, played in the streets or in the park until we were called home for supper. In many respects it was a typical, mainly happy, working-class life and it would have played out for me, I imagine, in a similar way to how it has for many of my school friends. I couldn't have followed my dad down the pit, of course, because that world changed so I'm not sure what I would have ended up doing. I don't think it would have been what I'm doing now though.

Two things happened to change the tenor of that life. Firstly, my dad, in his words, 'woke up to his potential' and realised that he had an innate intelligence, without formal qualification, and was a good deal more talented than what was being asked of him as a collier working on the coal face of a pit. This fostered in him an ambition, at forty years old, to use these skills, to get qualified and to go into higher management. Unlike the 'rude forefathers' of Grey's churchyard, he was offered an opportunity to develop himself because the National Coal Board had a programme for people just like my dad. He succeeded in his ambition by taking a Higher National Diploma at technical college in the evenings and on day release (at the same time and on the same course as his 21-year-old son-in-law) and by proving his ability at work and securing a manager's job. Looking back, what a role model of aspiration this was and what an example of what this aspiration combined with the right opportunity can lead to.

The second event that changed the tenor of things for me was that to secure his management position, as a family we had to move to another mining village fifty miles away and I started a new secondary school that gave me some of the unhappiest years of my life but also gave me the determination to change things up for myself much as my dad had for his family.

One of the later chapters covers the story of my coming to terms with my sexuality in a hostile environment, which it really was in the 1970s, so no need to cover it here. Suffice to say it was pretty brutal. Combine this with a shockingly poor quality of education provided by the secondary school, I only just managed to scrape together sufficient qualifications to go to university, and it starts to give a flavour of what some of my drivers have been in my professional life. I look back on that schooling with anger, not particularly for myself, because any failings in the teaching were compensated for by both my mum and dad spending hours and hours teaching me the things I should have been learning at school, but for those who could have achieved so much more, could have had the opportunities I have subsequently had, if only the school had had ambition for them and done their job of educating us properly. It was bitter irony when years later I read about how many times the school had failed its inspections, generations of young people failed. Thank goodness it's a good school now, part of a multi-academy trust.

The decision to train as a teacher was an easy one, I've always loved being around children and the chance to make a difference to their lives has to be the greatest privilege. The irony is I almost didn't make it, so poor were my maths results, but I did eventually.

My career in education was a successful one, not dissimilar to many other peoples', and doesn't need detailing here. The factors that either helped or hindered it are covered in Chapter 10. It's a story of rapidly climbing the leadership ladder culminating, with a change in Government policy, in establishing REAch2 Multi Academy Trust and becoming its Chief Executive Officer. The subject of many of the reflections in this book.

I took a while in sharing my early life as it is precisely that experience that dictated, firstly, the types of schools that I have always worked in but also why I established REAch2 and, with the help of some very key people of course, built it into the largest primary Trust in the country.

If you look at the profile of the schools and the communities they serve you'll see a common denominator, children that need aspiration and need opportunity. You'll also see a lot of schools that previously were not giving children a good enough education, but they are now.

If we fast forward to today having stepped down after ten years as Chief Executive of REAch2, I do feel a bit like Thomas Grey, reflecting on any contribution I might have made to the children and communities I wanted to serve. In general, I am satisfied. Thousands of children are getting a good education in schools at the centre of their communities, the Trust invests and looks after its staff, there are initiatives that really nurture aspiration and provide exceptional opportunities and the organisation is fit for purpose. It will have an enduring impact.

It is in our nature as educationalists, though, to want to continue our own learning and support that of others. And so, to the 'Being the CEO' book and programme and now this book, 'Reflections on Being the CEO'

Michael Pain has been a long-time friend and colleague to me and those at REAch2. He was influential in the early days of establishing the Trust with everything from vision to governance and over the last ten years has been a trusted person to turn to for advice and guidance. His book 'Being the CEO' – which it is helpful to read alongside this one - is the seminal work on carrying out this role in the education sector and there is still nothing like it. Meanwhile, the Being the CEO programme which works with small groups of CEOs is making a really significant contribution to the professional learning of academy trust CEOs and it has been my privilege to support with the delivery of this programme, drawing upon my ten-year experience of carrying out the role.

I talk in the next chapter about my decision to step down as the CEO and what I want to do next. As well as the personal things, like travel more, I feel that having learnt so much over the last ten years in a sector that I feel passionately about, sharing some of that learning will, hopefully, be useful to those just undertaking the role or in the role and facing similar challenges. There is no doubt that the last ten years have been the most professionally challenging ones of my career and there have been real highs and lows and navigating the system and sector is almost an art form. In an educational context, the role of CEO is still relatively new and very much still in development and I'd like to be involved in shaping the thinking around this. Writing monthly blogs and basing them on the six dimensions contained within Michael's book seems to me a sensible, accessible and practical way of doing this.

In the mentoring of CEOs that I have undertaken since stepping down, it has quickly become apparent that many CEOs are finding the step up to being CEO, often from Executive Headship, a tricky one and many are slowly finding their way. It is equally clear that many are facing similar challenges. In each of the blogs I try to achieve a balance of lived experience, received wisdom and practical advice, it seems like common sense to offer common solutions to recurring challenges. One of the themes I return to in the blogs, is the importance of being yourself in being the CEO, of letting your personality shine through, so the blogs model this and are often quirky, contain anecdotes, literary allusions and personal reflections. I'm keen to ensure "Reflections on Being the CEO', offers practical advice and guidance too and so have added what I call 'winning moves' at the end of each chapter. These are simply three of four things that have worked for me on each theme, and I offer them to prompt thinking and reflection, not as a rule book.

Several months have passed since I stepped down as CEO and the perspective this has given has consolidated my belief that the key to success is mindset, once you embrace the mantle, you must think and act accordingly and do what only you can do: **BE** the CEO

I have really enjoyed writing 'Reflections on Being the CEO'. I hope you equally enjoy reading it.

1

What an Adventure!

'As a CEO, this is life as we know it, and the best way to deal with it is to focus on the end game as we know it.'

Sir Steve wrote the following blog shortly after standing down as Chief Executive of REAch2 Academy Trust after over a decade in post. In it he introduces a key theme that he comes back to frequently throughout the articles in this book: as a Chief Executive, whilst it is important to maintain a focus on the 'here and now', to deal with crisis with care, and to recognise that short-term, annual metrics will never go away; it is also essential to constantly balance this with a longer-term, bigger picture view of progress and success over time. This is especially important for maintaining one's resilience as CEO in any 'high stakes' sector with significant and varying degrees of oversight and accountability.

Sir Steve writes candidly about making the decision to step down as Chief Executive, recognising his place on Handy's interpretation of the Sigmoid curve of learning, growth and decline. 'Knowing thyself' as Chief Executive, and one's own strengths, weaknesses, and contribution to the organisation at its particular stage of development is a defining skill. There are times, he says, when "CEOs need to offer something different in our leadership to take the organisation to the next level."

Knowing thyself also means knowing your limits, whether that's in terms of knowledge, capacity, experience or expertise, and *recognising that as CEO you are very often not the right person to lead an aspect of the organisation's work - even if that work comes with great profile and influence. In these circumstances, swallowing ego, and taking the decision that is right for the organisation is a key litmus test for a successful Chief Executive. That said, and as he explores at length, CEOs must ensure they are doing 'CEO type things' and using their time, energy and focus on the areas that only they can influence and make happen.*

Sir Steve ends by reflecting on authenticity and being oneself in the CEO role, which ensures that those who follow us know who we really are and why, indeed, they should be led by us.

*****

'What an adventure!' said Alice. Sums up nicely my experience of the last ten years as founder and first Chief Executive of REAch2. It's a saying that we used widely across the Trust to either celebrate a positive outcome or lament something we really rather wish hadn't happened. It's used a bit like Kipling's 'If you can meet with triumph and disaster and treat those two imposters the same'. It's apt because after these ten years, if there's one thing I'm sure of, it is that as trust leaders we will experience the good and the bad. Years when results are great, inspections go well, schools get built and whatever is in our strategic plan gets delivered. Then there are those times when you fall down the rabbit hole and the world looks entirely different. A poor inspection, a nasty incident in a school, a major safeguarding issue, key staff leaving or something else that pushes us off centre. It took me a good few years to realise that, as a CEO, this is life as we know it, forever, and the best way to deal with it is to focus on the end game and not get embroiled in annual soul searching. Sure, reflect on the pros and cons of the year, but keep a sense of perspective and react proportionately to both imposters. It's a strategy that has helped me cope with this very difficult job we all do.

Adventure is not a word I use lightly as I reflect upon my own story of growth and development as a CEO. The (over?) regulated, highly accountable, risk averse system we find ourselves part of today is a world away from the 'Academy sector wild west' of ten years ago when I first called myself 'CEO' without having a clue what it really meant or entailed. It seems inconceivable now that trusts, and hence CEOs, would be put through beauty parades competing against each other to win the hearts and votes of governing bodies, or face angry and abusive communities enraged at 'forced' academisation. That a CEO could negotiate twelve sponsored academies in one year, all over the country, or bid for, and secure, twenty-two free schools in one go. It's not nostalgia that prompts me to offer this description of times gone by – because there is no way I'd want to return to it – more an explanation that my own journey as a CEO is probably atypical. Nevertheless, I hope these reflections on 'What worked for me' will be helpful to colleagues currently in the role.

It's a month now since I handed over the CEO baton and the most frequent question I've been asked is 'How do you feel?' Easy! A mixture of pride, relief and excitement. I'm proud of the organisation I helped build. I won't bore you with too many details, but sixteen thousand children are now in a good or better school that weren't previously, that starting from a base of 9% of its schools being good, the trust now has 96% of schools good or better, and that a recent staff survey showed 96% of staff in our schools feel they are well respected, well looked after, and are happy. The relief comes from – it's a tough job, you never stop worrying about it, it can be all-consuming and, at times, very lonely.

There are also those 'rabbit holes' I mention above that come along to test us to our limit. There are two particularly memorable ones for me, (which are by no means of equal magnitude). Firstly, the Education Skills and Funding Agency deciding that the whole REAch2 structure of umbrella trust over ten MATs was illegal, issuing us with a notice of dissolution, and threatening legal action against the CEO (!). And secondly, very early on, a real time phone call with one of our directors who was on site at an inspection asking what to do as a parent was smoking pot outside the inspectors' window. (Waft it away and move them on was the best I could come up with). Whilst it is the most professionally rewarding role I've ever done, there is a sense of 'My part in this story is done, time for someone else to shoulder the responsibility'.

The best part is the excitement I feel on two fronts. Firstly, the Trust is in good hands, and I don't need to worry about it, but also, selfishly,

I can now throw myself into what I equally love doing; supporting and mentoring other Chief Executives and Executive Leaders, helping organisations grow and develop, and giving back to a sector that has given me so much. It's why I was delighted that Michael Pain and Alice Gregson offered me the opportunity both to Chair Forum Strategy's National CEO network and mentor on the 'Being the CEO' programme. Michael was the first person to recognise that the sector needed this kind of support and I wish I'd had his book and programme ten years ago. Similarly, what a privilege to be part of such a tremendous network of CEOs, and I hope as Chair of the network I can offer something of value.

So, on to what's worked for me. Two things I'd like to focus on in this blog. 'Being' the CEO in terms of knowing yourself, knowing what value you bring to the organisation and being an authentic CEO, and then on 'Doing CEO type things', which is about what we actually do or should be doing in our role.

On the first, CEO know thyself. There are two good reasons that I've stepped down now and not in five- or ten-years' time as I could have done. I'm a big believer in the Sigmoid curve and Handy's interpretation of it. Under this, organisations and, I would suggest, people (AKA CEOs) go through three phases: the learning phase, growth phase, and the decline phase. According to Hardy, the success of an organisation is linked to being aware of where they are on the curve, between growth and decline, and doing something about it at the right time before decline sets in. That 'something' might be organisations reinventing themselves or doing something radically different. I would suggest that this applies to us all as CEOs too and it is about the relative value we add to our organisation, particularly over time. Since we are the highest paid, we should consistently add the most value.

The 'Being the CEO' programme is very much about this first phase and is a respectable recognition that for many the role of CEO is relatively new and, as such, we are obliged to learn as much as we can, to become as knowledgeable and capable as we are able. This is as it should be and will last a certain amount of time. The challenge, I think, is when the organisation is at that point where initial growth has taken place, incremental improvement has gone as far as it can go, and where our well-tried strategies and 'business as usual' activity only does so much. Where we, as CEOs, need to offer something different in our leadership to take the organisation to the next level. A key skill, I believe, is in recognising this point and, as Handy says, doing something about it. This might be in changing organisational strategy, developing new ways of working, branching out into a new sector, or bringing fresh ideas into the executive team. The CEO network can provoke us and help us develop connections that – as established CEOs – give us important value in this regard.

Last year (2021), given our shared experience of the pandemic and reflecting on how best to continue to serve our school communities, I realised that REAch2 was at that point on the Sigmoid curve, and I was at that point in my CEO tenure, where we both should do something entirely different. My choice was to reinvent myself or leave. The decision for me to step down was, I hope, an honest recognition that there were people better placed to take the Trust forward, people who could add more value. Honest evaluation of what value we add as CEO doesn't, of course, need to end in stepping down, but it does require action on our part, and it's a question I think we all should ask ourselves at intervals.

The second dimension to 'know thyself' which has helped me is the understanding that leadership needs to be about collective capacity and efficacy and not personal status; knowing when to put the job title aside and let someone else lead something or do something because they are better at it has served me well. For example, unusually, I was not the Accounting Officer for REAch2 because I have a problem understanding figures, spreadsheets, statistics, numbers; I've struggled my whole life with it. I coped for a while but as the organisation got bigger and the numbers larger, I couldn't put my hand on my heart and say I could be an effective Accounting Officer and give the Board etc. the assurance they needed. Swallowing ego and acknowledging that the Chief Operating Officer, a trained accountant, was much better placed to do this, and securing agreement for this to happen was one of the best decisions I ever made. So much better for the organisation and all concerned to get an expert to do it.

Of course, there had to be absolute trust between us, and it is a bit of a deficit (no pun intended) model, but it brought home to me that my real job as CEO was to make the organisation as effective as possible by allowing those most skilled and capable to do the job at hand. This helped us all as an Executive team reframe our thinking about who did what and think about what I now call 'best placed leadership'. There are numerous examples at every level of the Trust now where job title has been put aside, and those best placed to lead something, lead it. To me it's not about someone not being able to do their job, it is about securing excellence, releasing potential and utilising, in full, collective capacity.

The final bit of 'Being' the CEO is about being authentic. I personally value this above all else and I see it in two ways; being true to yourself – and being yourself – and they are different. For me, authenticity is the extent to which what a person believes is consistently reflected in what they say and what they do, and one of the factors central to any notion of authenticity must surely be consistency, both over time and across different situations. I think there are three variables at play here; the integration and interaction of values, language, and actions, in a way that demonstrates integrity and trustworthiness. We only have to look at our government in May 2022 to see what happens to authenticity and trust when actions don't match words (or laws) and what people say they value is not borne out in their actions.

My approach to this has been to externalise my values i.e. tell everyone, everywhere across the organisation what I believe and hold dear and invite them to challenge me if they think I'm not being consistent with them. It has happened a couple of times and I've welcomed it. I think this in itself builds trust and credibility. On being yourself, the biggest thing I mentor new CEOs on is how to relax, let people see the real you, and not worry too much about what people think. The best CEOs, I think, have the confidence to do this and realise that consistent values, language and action will make sure people form the right impression and will ensure authenticity. Who doesn't love a bit of sparkle? So let that personality shine, I say. People will follow you to the end of the earth if they know you are genuine and you bring colour to their professional life.

On to my second reflection, if there's one thing I feel very strongly about it's that the CEO should do 'CEO type things'. As I've become a more mature and, hopefully, more effective CEO, it's something that I've given a lot of thought to and, in the last few years, committed, through self-discipline to putting into action. I recognise, of course, that it's contextual and circumstances vary and that it's usually tied to size and capacity, but the CEO really ought to be focusing on all things strategic and getting out of the weeds of management and, even worse, administration. I have always found distinguishing between these three things a helpful exercise in deciding where to focus effort and attention. A few years ago, John-West Burnham, in our coaching, helped me bring clarity to the inter-relation and difference between these three things and encouraged me to see them as a continuum (with leadership activity on the left and administration on the right) and devised a model to exemplify.

In this approach, the difference between the three is exemplified in terms of the principle of each activity, the purpose and how this involves people. In this model, Leadership defines the values, the purpose and secures the engagement of stakeholders (people), Management translates principle into consistent practice, and Administration ensures organisational neatness. As far as the principle is concerned, Leadership is 'doing the right things', Management is 'doing things right' and administration is simply 'doing things'.

	Leadership	Management	Administration
Principle	Doing the right things	Doing things right	Doing things
Purpose	Path making	Path following	Path tidying
People	Engaging with complexity	Creating clarity	Securing consistency

The Purpose of leadership is 'path making', of Management 'path following' and Administration' path tidying' and finally, in terms of people, Leadership engages with the complexity of stakeholders, Management creates clarity and administration secures consistency. The challenge which John rightly presented me with was 'How much time are you spending on each activity?' because, he argued, 'the more time you spend on the left of the continuum, the better CEO you will be and the more likely you are to succeed in realising your ambitions, and the more on the right, the less effective your Trust will be and, to be blunt, the less effective you will be as a CEO'.

He was right, and it led me to really question everything I did each week, month and year. This view is supported by most research into CEO effectiveness and I was always minded by the McKinsey research which found that the distinction between good CEOs and great CEOs is the ability to focus. Great CEOs play the 'big game', they focus on the top 3-5 most important initiatives and they dedicate 90% of their time, energy and resources to these. The say 'no' often and they don't allow their time to fill up with different activities and different priorities. Less effective CEOs are weaker at prioritisation, allow their time to be filled up with other things (management and administration), and fit in the important initiatives around the 'day job'. I support the view that great CEOs delegate the running of the Trust to an effective executive or leadership team. They make themselves unnecessary to the day-to-day operation of the Trust so that they can focus on the future.

Jeff Bezos apparently says he spends 5% of his time running his company. I didn't quite get to that point, but a fair estimate would be that over the last five years I spent a good 85% of my time on leading the Trust (setting strategy, securing alignment, leading the executive team, managing talent, protecting the culture, engaging with the Board and other stakeholders) and not managing it or 'tidying up'. I think it's one of the reasons that we responded to the challenges of the pandemic so well and are in as strong a position as we have ever been. People I work with will quote a phrase I often say (I think it's mine and I haven't assimilated it from somewhere else). 'The quality and effectiveness of your organisation will be directly proportionate to the quality of your thinking about it'. CEOs think more than they do. Over to you!

WINNING MOVES

∞ Answer your own 'legacy question' by beginning at the end. What will the organisation look like and be like when your tenure is over? What will constitute success? Write your own description or draw a mind map so that you know what you are striving for. This will help keep annual or short-term ups and downs in perspective and give you a hint when your job is done and it's time to move on.

∞ Be intentional in being authentic. Make your own values and beliefs explicit by sharing them at regular intervals and invite people in the organisation to hold you to account in how your language and behaviours match up to them. Remember that authenticity comes from being human, allow your personality to shine through but keep a slight sense of mystery and throw in a few surprises at times.

∞ Be disciplined in being strategic. 'Notice' the types of activities you spend most time on and each week, month, year ask yourself if you're being a leader, a manager or an administrator. Keep a log even on how you spend your time. Invite colleagues to remind you to get out of the weeds and onto the balcony and remember that thinking is probably the most important leadership activity you can do.

∞ Know the three things that are critical to the success of your organisation or will make the most positive difference and make them 'your things'. Focus on them with laser-like intent and use your influence as CEO to make sure they are on everyone's agenda.

2

A New Kind of CEO?

'CEOs will need to bring a greater degree of hope. We will need - with the board - a clearer vision of how we will navigate this volatile, changing, turbulent world, and we will need a more compelling narrative.'

This particular blog focuses on some of the key themes within dimension one of the Being the CEO framework - the importance of developing a compelling leadership narrative that brings people with us. However, it also extends beyond it to consider the evolution of the Chief Executive role in recent years. Sir Steve wrote the blog in June 2022 following the (now) annual National #TrustLeaders Symposium, where he was joined by Sir Michael Barber, former Head of the Prime Minister's Delivery Unit under Tony Blair, and Maggie Farrar in leading a day of big picture thinking and networking amongst CEOs. The event was attended by almost two hundred trust executive leaders. At the forefront of his mind when writing the piece was the ambition of those in the audience to make a profound difference for their pupils and communities in what were uncertain and challenging times following the pandemic and the onset of the cost-of-living crisis.

In the blog, Sir Steve approaches the topics of visioning and setting strategy, recognising that VUCA (volatility, uncertainty, complexity and ambiguity) is here to stay. He writes of how the role of CEO is shifting as a result. Whilst prerequisites such as strategic vision, domain specific expertise, financial acumen, people skills (such as empathy, understanding), clarity of thought, determination, focus and drive remain, he now also considers it essential for Chief Executives (and boards) to embark upon the task of leadership by constantly listening to and learning from those at all levels of their organisation, and looking outwards to their communities and to wider society in order to help set direction. In doing so CEOs can enhance their ability to be adaptable and responsive, avoiding sticking to outdated or redundant strategic and financial plans, and refining strategy and shaping an evolving narrative that connects with and inspires those around them, meeting our end users' needs in the process. The world is moving too fast and growing in such complexity for CEOs not to build this into their leadership approach.

Sir Steve goes on to explore how CEOs we will need to embrace uncertainty and learn how to live with it - demonstrating resilience and generating a sense of stability and clarity. Alongside this he advocates for an inclusive approach to distributing and involving others in leadership, not least where expertise and knowledge exists elsewhere across the organisation and beyond it; and the fundamental importance of demonstrating humility and a deep-seated curiosity in a complex and unpredictable world.

****

I truly enjoyed our National #TrustLeaders Symposium this week and meeting so many CEOs, COOs, and Education Executives from across Forum Strategy's networks and memberships. The theme of 'Accomplishment' was well timed, because, however you define that term, the fact that we were all together in the same room talking about bold aspirations for trusts' futures (and the trust sector's future!) means that we had already accomplished something fairly significant. We have weathered a mighty storm and are now looking to the future – together; that is an accomplishment in itself.

The pandemic has been brutal in its impact on individuals, on society and on our work as trust leaders. Our communities have suffered, many of us have suffered on a personal level, and society in general has suffered in so many ways. And yet, here we are this week, talking and planning for a brighter future and challenging ourselves and each other as trust leaders to do better and to do more. To be the answer to so many questions and the solution to so many problems. This gives me tremendous hope and it emphasises the potential for doing good that sits with us as trust leaders. We have a pivotal role to play in ensuring our schools and our communities come back stronger and even better equipped to tackle what's in front of us next.

This question of what's in front of us is such an interesting one. Without being alarmist, I think our world has changed. And because it has changed, what is expected of us has changed and what we need to deliver on is different too. The pandemic showed that schools are the 'go to' places for families and communities that are struggling, that we are trusted to be a constant in an uncertain world, and that we are in the incredibly privileged position of being able to make a real difference to so many lives.

What has changed for Chief Executives and for our organisations?

Firstly, the context in which we operate has changed. Our experience over the last couple of years has shown that we have less certainty in how life will be, of what we will have to face, and that the good old VUCA (Volatility, Uncertainty, Complexity and Ambiguity) factor will intensify in the future. Without putting too fine a point on it, the short term will become increasingly unpredictable for us, I think, and the long term virtually unknowable.

In addition to this, it's clear that certain issues have become increasingly pressing for society at large and therefore need to be high on our agenda. Four in particular spring to mind – the increased emphasis, reliance and potential of AI technology; the focus on environmental issues and sustainability; socio-political issues centred on diversity, inclusion and equity; and the absolute necessity of protecting and promoting wellbeing. Towards the end of last year, as a Trust, we held virtual drop ins with key stakeholders (Head teachers, staff, parents, children etc.); we also surveyed them. The purpose was to ask what was important to them in the here and now, and therefore, what the priorities of the Trust should be going forward. The responses were completely different compared to those given when the same exercise was carried out pre-pandemic and, by and large, centred around the factors listed above. This demonstrated to me that what is important to our community right now has shifted and I realised that if we are to serve our community as we ought, then our priorities should change too. I threw our five-year plan in the bin.

It also prompted me to ask a different question though; a rather tricky one. If what's needed from a trust has changed, to deal with this uncertain, volatile, re-prioritised world, has what's needed from its leader changed? In fact, to go to the extreme, going forward, is a new type of CEO needed?

I've given some thought to this, and – without wishing to fudge the question – the answer is both yes and no. Let me explain. A good CEO is traditionally associated with certain key qualities: strategic vision, domain specific expertise, financial acumen, people skills (such as empathy, understanding), clarity of thought, determination, focus, drive, and so on. These are, of course, still prerequisites, and in the future some of the leadership attributes that have served us well to date are still going to be of utmost importance going forward. I was reminded of this recently. For those of you on Twitter you will have seen that I've spent the last two months visiting all the schools in the REAch2 family. A goodbye tour. In all these visits two things have emerged. Firstly, the need for reassurance that life in a world without the founder CEO will be ok (yes, it will!). And secondly (and more importantly), the worries and anxieties of many head teachers centred around this question; 'we signed up to your vision, will we stay true to that?' I can't, of course, answer that; it's no longer in my gift to say 'yes'. But it did reinforce the importance of that compelling vision, both to people within and outside of the organisation. So, it's always been needed and not new.

My favourite description of vision (amongst the very many) is 'a picture of the future that fulfils a deep hope within us'. I like this because I believe everyone in our schools has hope – we are that kind of sector. We go into teaching, go on to become leaders, become CEOs, because we hope we can make a difference. We hope we can make the world a better place for the children in our care, hope we can prepare them to succeed whatever the future holds. So, whilst this is not new, I do believe that going forward, because of our experience of the last few years, CEOs will need to bring a *greater* degree of hope. We will need a clearer vision of how we will navigate this volatile, changing, turbulent world, and we will need a more compelling narrative. The work at the symposium on bold ambition was a great start to this and it will need to be a golden thread running through all that we do as CEOs and leaders. Let's plant the idea of hopeful leadership, a theme we will focus in detail on at the Forum CEO conference in September.

What does this mean for how we operate as Chief Executives?

So, if providing and constantly reaffirming a compelling vision is something a good CEO has always done and just needs to do more of, and be more compelling in going forward, why would I think that something new is needed?

One reason is that the classic approach we have always taken to trust, school or any organisational development won't work anymore, or at least not in the same way. It's always been fairly straightforward: set a five-year strategy, spend three years delivering on that strategy, then start to plan the next cycle (some of you might have worked on a three-year strategy but the principle is the same). I think for the next generation of CEOs, that tried and tested process is far less relevant because those timescales won't work – change will be continuous, disruption possible (even likely) and uncertainty will become a way of life. Just take a look at all the things that are currently the reality of our lives: the cost-of-living crisis, political unrest, global conflict etc. etc. These haven't suddenly emerged from nowhere, of course, but they weren't in my plan five years ago. Any good CEO can't ignore them or we risk failing to serve our communities in the way they need.

This has real implications for how a CEO will need to operate. Firstly, we will need to embrace uncertainty and learn how to live with it. Again, we touched on this theme at the symposium. It's an uncomfortable feeling, more so for some than others depending upon our nature, but it will become a significant factor, I believe, and we will need a greater degree of resilience to cope with it. We will need to find ways of bringing calm, stability and clarity of thought to this uncertain environment. We will also need to be more cognisant than ever of our wellbeing and ability to self-restore in the face of this more challenging context.

Secondly, in this environment, CEOs of today and tomorrow will need to be more adaptable, flexible and creative. They will need to be able to shift gear and change direction at speed. The pandemic showed us the necessity of this, I think in the future other things will too. I read a phrase recently that explained this beautifully – we will need the ability to perform and transform. Which means combining short term responsiveness with long term strategy. I used a phrase at the symposium that the story of REAch2 was one of building the plane whilst flying it; it's a similar concept and I think will become more of a reality for all of us as we have to adapt to external influences beyond our control. This may be a different way of working for many and we need to consider how well we are equipped (and comfortable) with dealing with it.

Another significant implication is that in the future I think traditional roles and structure will need to change and we will need an evolved view of leadership in this context and an evolved view of the role of the CEO. Hierarchical, centralised structures centred on positional authority are a thing of the past. We have all come a long way in this already but we will need to go further. The complexity of the challenges facing us as CEOs means that we will need to leverage the collective leadership capacity of the organisation a lot more than we ever have. Leadership cannot sit with just a few people and CEOs will need to be ever more willing to share the leadership mantle. This will bring with it flattened structures, even more distributed leadership and an executive team which will function closer to equals with more focus on delivery and impact and less focus on roles and titles. A collective shouldering of responsibility. In this, CEOs will need to put ego aside and embrace the fact that we do not need to be the best in the team, but to have the best team. This will take confidence. Sir Michael's phrase of 'releasing the music in people' so resonated with my own view that as CEOs we need to focus on the 'availability of leadership' across an organisation and that it is about collective capacity and not personal authority. In the future a CEO's ability to hear and release the potential of those voices wherever they may be in the organisation will be crucial.

To touch on the four themes I mentioned earlier, in no particular order or rank of importance. A trend that is going to continue to dominate the educational landscape in the future is technological change. Technology already impacts on most facets of our organisations: day to day functioning, communication, teaching and learning and so on. Many of us really went up a gear in this respect (though it was still a challenge) when we had to make a relatively simple shift to remote learning during the pandemic. Technology has also become such a dominant force in our pupils' lives, and their ability to use it as a force for good, and with creativity and purpose, will now define their life chances to a great extent. Continual technological advances mean that it will become even more pervasive and important in the future. Most CEOs in industry are seeing this as the 'Fourth Industrial Revolution' where automation, online learning and services and even AI will become dominant.

I'm not suggesting that children will suddenly need to be taught by robots (if this were true, I would choose Marvin from Hitchhiker's guide to the Galaxy – how's the exams going Steve? Badly I feel!), but it does mean that, moving forward, CEOs and other leaders will need to have stronger technological skills so they can use the digital world to the best advantage. Just look at how social media has become so dominant. This is just the start of it and being ahead of the curve in this respect is going to be really important. We are already seeing some trusts responding to this by appointing Chief Digital Officers (we are just about to do this at REAch2) and going back to my point earlier, these Chief Digital Officers will become as important as any other executive in leading the organisation, and as CEOs we must be comfortable with and embrace this.

Recently, I was really struck by a comment in a book that I'm reading on social responsibility. It's looking at social responsibility in a corporate world, not educational, but it still holds, I think. The quote is *'there is a changing of the guard at CEO level. Fewer big egos and grandees and many more individuals who lead with humility and are prepared to be held more accountable than ever before on the impact their business has on society and the planet.'* Given what I said earlier about schools being the centre of their communities and the go to place (and thus influencer) for many, the need for CEOs to become societal leaders as well as trust leaders is ever growing. I believe new CEOs, and those in the role right now, will need to really embrace this and examine how the work we do really tackles the issues of diversity, inclusion, and equity, not just within our trusts, but in our wider communities and society at large. We will also need to look more forensically, given the fourth emergent theme, at how the work we do addresses environmental issues and sustainability. For many, these will have been on the agenda for a while. I think the pandemic and what's happening in the world right now has escalated these themes to the top of everyone's agenda. The question is (back to the symposium) how bold can we be in our ambition in tackling them? This is the challenge CEOs now and going forward need to answer.

Let's embrace the opportunity here

I think my final reflection, going back to my own question, is that there is no doubt the successful CEOs of the future will need to differ in mindset, skillset and approach from the CEO of the past. The world has changed and will continue to change and what will be demanded from the role will only increase in complexity. We will still need some of those abilities traditionally associated with the role, like telling that compelling narrative and winning hearts and minds to an ambitious vision, but to my mind, given all we have said above, we must evolve in the role. This shouldn't frighten us though. Our response to it needs to be that we will prepare ourselves for this. To embrace it and see it for what is – *an opportunity to carve out a stronger, more impactful, more fulfilling role than ever.*

WINNING MOVES

∞ Be a powerful storyteller. Develop your own compelling narrative about what you do as an organisation and why you do it. Constantly reaffirm this. Describe the better future that exists from your perspective using anecdotes, stories, memories. Develop a common language and use shared history to build a sense of common 'identity'. Take time to explain to people what part they play and why they are important to the story.

∞ Make 'Are you being served?' the most frequent question you ask. Develop both formal and informal ways to regularly consult with key stakeholders to make sure that your organisation's priorities are closely aligned with the needs of those you are there to support. Rely more heavily on informal, frequent consultation than procedural and mechanistic processes and systems. You'll get more fidelity.

∞ Adopt 'habits of hope' as part of your leadership strategy and be that person who brings a sense of optimism. Develop a mindset that sees opportunities rather than problems, that values kindness. Remember that you are the rock on which all waves crash, people need to believe this, so adopt a persona that engenders confidence and steadfastness, especially in tough times, especially when you least feel it.

3

Word Play and Board Games

'In every relationship, though, the central tenet is always going to be centred on trust.'

This blog focuses on some of the key themes within the second dimension of the *Being the CEO* framework - the all-important relationship between the CEO and the board, with a particular focus on the relationship with the Chair.

Sir Steve wrote this article shortly after the publication of Forum Strategy's initial think piece in its series of work on 'Thriving Trusts'. He considers the importance of words and language in leadership, and the need for leaders to consider the connotations, and to be intentional, around the words they choose to use with others. The language of 'thriving', he says, reflects a sense of growth and evolution.

To the main topic, Sir Steve writes on the huge influence that the quality of the board and the relationship with the Chair of Trustees had upon his growth and success as a Chief Executive. The foundation, he writes, is trust and trust is forged through good experiences. Linked to that, there is a need for shared understanding and demarcation of roles and responsibilities, openness and transparency, and mutual respect. It is, as Sir Steve writes, not unlike a marriage.

****

"Words are, in my not-so-humble opinion, our most inexhaustible source of magic. Capable of both inflicting injury and remedying it. "

Yes indeed, Dumbledore. Well said. I've long been a student of the power of language and sometimes obsess excessively over choice of words both when speaking and (especially) when writing. Not in a *Pride and Prejudice* Mr Collins kind of way ('I do sometimes amuse myself with arranging such little elegant compliments, I always wish to give them as unstudied an air as possible') but more in an appreciation of their importance in ensuring that the intention behind whatever is spoken or written is delivered with clarity, without ambiguity and leaves as little to (mis)interpretation as possible.

I read a study a while ago about the words that powerful people avoid because they can diminish message and intent. Words such as 'just' – which is a protector word, softening what needs to be achieved (I'm just following up on..) and playing down the importance of what you are seeking or doing; drama words – such as 'totally', 'absolutely' (I'm totally committed..) which can be superfluous and add unnecessary drama and reduce the impact of a message or comment; superior words – such as 'actually' and 'obviously', which can be condescending and seem to make assumptions about a person's level of understanding; and finally, ability words ('I'll try' or 'don't worry about it') which can suggest that you are unsure of your abilities or lack confidence or, with the second phrase, are overconfident and are belittling the other person. When I read it, it really resonated because I do pay close attention to what people say and write, and the language they choose to use. And make assumptions based on it.

In a completely different way, I love some words because they are just fun to say – words that take your mouth to the gym so that when you've enunciated every syllable you've done the oral equivalent of a bench press or a drop set (I believe those are gym terms!). Two such words are 'nomenclature' and 'gubernatorial' which, happily, are pertinent to the theme of this blog. Before we get to that, just have a go (slowly) and you'll see what I mean.

No-men-cla-ture (nəʊˈmeŋ.klə.tʃə)
Gu-ber-naˈto-ri-al (guː.bən.əˈtɔː.ri.əl)

See? And just like after any gym workout, you've earned a glass of wine. These phonetically pleasing words are pertinent in different ways, and I'll come to the second one a little later on.

Nomenclature has its origins in early 17th century French and Latin. Nomenclatura from nomen 'name' and clatura 'calling' and means, of course, (please mentally delete 'of course', it's a superior word) a name applied to something. So, what naming ceremony has been happening to catch my eye? None other than our very own Forum Strategy publishing its first thinkpiece on 'Thriving Trusts'. And in doing so rejecting the nomenclature that both the DfE (and other organisations) have adopted in using the term 'Strong Trusts'. But is this just semantics and to be ignored? I don't think so. I do have a problem with the notion of a 'strong' trust and I am much (remove 'much' – drama word!) more comfortable with the more sophisticated 'thriving'. Why?

Firstly, let's put aside for now the connotations of power, autocracy and even force, closely associated with 'strong', (you can be strong and evil as well as strong and good); to me, using 'strong trust' implies that there is a fixed descriptor that can be applied to a trust. That we can write a list of characteristics that, just like the Ofsted framework, tries to capture what 'strong' looks like and when you've ticked all the boxes you get the badge. We all know this one size fits all, mechanistic approach does little to capture the richness and complexity of our schools; it'll do even less to properly capture the diverse nature of organisations, structured in a myriad of ways, serving a wide range of communities, of different sizes and in different stages of development.

There are two possible reasons for wanting to categorise trusts in this way. One is an attempt to identify and share best practice; the other, if I was cynical enough to say it, is to provide a 'framework' to hold trusts accountable by regulators. My view is the former, whilst laudable, won't be achieved in this way, it is too unsophisticated to properly describe the nature and effectiveness of what trusts do, and as for the latter, that already exists in the form of summary evaluations by HMI, which to be fair are generally conducted well and I have had only positive experiences of.

My main reason, though, for preferring the idea of 'thriving trusts' is that, by definition, it acknowledges that we are in a period of trust evolution. At the time of writing, the oldest registered academy trust in the country is just over twenty years old with the vast majority being much younger. Compare that to the oldest registered company in the world (generally regarded as Kongō Gumi founded in 578, so well over 1400 years ago; a family-owned business in the construction sector building Buddhist temples) and we are reminded of just how young the sector is, and that maturation is, in my view, still a long way off. If we think of the generally recognised five stages of organisational/business growth, many trusts are still in the set up/developmental and growth stages in their evolution and I think this needs acknowledging in any attempt to either evaluate trusts, or when getting into the terms that best describe them. (Before we leave nomenclature, let's hope we never get into other business lifecycle terminology such as Zombie MATs or Dead MATs, it was bad enough having a conversation with a former Junior Minister about why I wouldn't set up a 'Hospital MAT').

Given all I've just said about the need to allow the sector to mature before drawing hard and fast conclusions, of course it's right for us to try and extrapolate what we can to this point. Some essential truths are emerging and I'm looking forward to the further work Forum Strategy is going to be doing in this area. I think it will be fascinating to see the correlation between conclusions being drawn in the academy trust sector and those more established lessons drawn from the wider business community. I'd expect to see a lot of commonality and one area that I'm particularly pleased to see identified as one of the six key areas in the Forum thinkpiece is the importance of shared governance at both Board level and local governing body level in generating greater support, accountability, and professional and social capital.

And so, to the second of my 'work out' words, gubernatorial. To many this will appear to be an Americanism, and indeed I first came across it when the Chair of Governors in my first Headship asked to see me on gubernatorial business and I had to fake it and then look it up! She was American and as it was second nature for her to use it, so it has become for me. It refers of course, in this sense, to the role of the trust board and other layers of governance in our organisations. As we know, collectively trusts have chosen to organise this in several different ways, the variation largely occurring around local governance and whether this has any real teeth through schemes of delegation or is advisory in nature. There's arguments for both, I always landed on the former because I'm a believer in local representation, local decision making and local accountability.

This aspect is not really what I'm going to focus on, however, because when considering 'thriving trusts' I am in no doubt that a good proportion of any success at REAch2 was down to gubernatorial effectiveness. Firstly, as a result of having a highly qualified, highly knowledgeable, brave trust board and secondly because of the quality of the relationship I was able to forge with each of the three Chairs of the Board who served during my tenure, as a result of which I was challenged and supported into being a better Chief Executive.

As far as the former is concerned, it's well documented what the benefits to an organisation are of having a top-notch board for the 'mechanics' of good corporate governance, compliance, regulation etc. Beyond this, the real additional value lay for me in our board's willingness to stand tall and be accountable, shoulder to shoulder with me when the stakes were high, when things didn't go as planned or when there were tough decisions to be taken. This gave me confidence and reassurance in their ability to encourage and even inspire innovation, whilst balancing this with skilful evaluation of potential risks to the trust. This kept us ambitious and creative yet safe and, despite them collectively being my boss, making their collective intellect, talent, skills, experience and knowledge open to me without any judgement, or ever making me feel inadequate or ill equipped for the job. It's quite something to work for such a team, and I choose that word carefully.

Much of this was possible, as I mentioned above, because of the relationship I formed with the Chair of the Board. It would've been easy to have been intimidated by the first Chair of REAch2. A Russell Group educated, highly successful, multi-millionaire businessman with a social conscience. Posh, rich and kind as I now, with his knowledge, fondly refer to him. I was in the strange position, as founder, of building a trust board and agreeing to them rather than the other way around. When I first met Peter, the Chair, and realised how impressive he was, and how challenging he might be, it would have been easy for the organisation and members/board to let him pass by (the DfE had put him forward from Academy Ambassadors) but there was something in his passion and commitment that seemed to mirror my own and when he said "I'm not looking to invest, but I will give endlessly of my time and experience", I realised that he was just what we needed in a Chair. Someone who knew more than me about running a company because, as a Head teacher of one primary school, I knew precious little about building an organisation to match the scale of my (and Peter's) ambition.

The rest is history. Peter and I were a perfect team seeing the organisation grow from one school to thirty schools in three years (thirty to sixty schools came with two different Chairs), the establishment of a second trust in a different part of the country (Astrea) and then a third (ReachSouth) and various other things. So, as I say, the perfect team. Sharing what made it so, will, I hope, be of interest to you as fellow CEOs in considering your own relationship, and the importance of this relationship, with the Chair of the Board. I've got two bits of 'home grown' wisdom to share.

Firstly, treat the relationship with the Chair of the Board like a marriage – and get a prenup! It is akin to a marriage - two people enter into an agreement accepting legal, financial (and emotional) responsibility for a family made up of adults, children, money, and property. Sound familiar? And like a marriage the entire family is affected when the relationship is in trouble; little can be accomplished in an organisation should the relationship between the CEO and Chair crumble. So how to prevent this?

A prenup conversation is really helpful in getting things off on the right footing. Ideally this conversation should happen before both parties start to work together, (as I did with Peter before appointment), but if that's not possible, as soon after as possible (as I did with the two subsequent Chairs following their election). The conversation needs to determine the practices that will best support the relationship. Each time, we focussed on expectations of each other, preferred methods of communication, preferred working patterns and an explicit promise to be open, transparent, and honest with each other.

The first building block of a successful relationship in this context, I believe, is mutual respect. Every CEO and Chair brings different experiences, beliefs, culture, and values to the table. Respecting and celebrating these differences and understanding the strength that this brings to the partnership is crucial. I genuinely valued Peter's immense commercial, entrepreneurial, business acumen. I also couldn't fail to admire his social conscience in giving so freely and genuinely of his time to our trust when he could have been doing a thousand other things. He tells me that he respected my achievements as an educationalist, my ambition to do more for disadvantaged communities and my passion for the role. So far so good. A mutual respect as equals that fosters a desire to make the partnership work.

In every relationship, though, the central tenet is always going to be centred on trust. Can each party trust each other, because we all know that without trust any relationship is doomed to failure. One of my Gurus, Michael Fullan, says that 'trust comes from good experiences'. I've always found this to be true and happily this has been the case for me. But it didn't happen by chance.

As Chair, Peter was very explicit with me in our prenup conversation about what I needed to do and how I needed to behave in order for him to trust me. In a very brief summary: no surprises, no hiding of mistakes or problems, no defensiveness, complete transparency and no bullshit. I was equally clear to him: don't interfere with the day job, tell me if you think I'm not doing something well enough, manage the board well and have my back (with the number of risks I took and some hefty mistakes I made, I tested this latter aspect to the limit). But we never let each other down; we were both true to our word and the trust benefited enormously from this. I was a better CEO; he was a better Chair.

The second piece of wisdom is to make sure there is role clarity between you both and to protect that distinction fiercely. If the roles are not clear then the relationship can be put in jeopardy. The job of the Chair is to run the board. The job of the CEO is to run the organisation. No confusion. I didn't really have an issue with this (the prenup worked on all three occasions).

In mentoring sessions with CEOs, though, I'm often surprised and sometimes a little alarmed when I hear about Chairs getting amongst the weeds of the day to day running of the organisation or being part of decision making at an operational level and not keeping that oh so important balcony view.

My advice to CEOs in this situation is, always have the confidence to tell them (nicely) to butt out. To be blunt, it does nobody any favours to indulge a Chair who wants to blur the boundaries. It works the other way too of course; it is incumbent on us as CEOs to know the limitations of our authority and understand when it is imperative to involve the Chair and indeed other trustees, and to accept that the Chair has an absolute right, in the right forum, to represent the trust without the CEO. Knowing these boundaries on both sides is key to an effective relationship that allows both parties to carry out their roles effectively, which is to the benefit of all.

So, to conclude. It is up to the sector, and all of us who are part of the sector, to take control of the narrative around what thriving trusts look like. It's not for a politician, a civil servant or anyone else who hasn't done the job.

We are the people perfectly positioned to make the case that the best way to fulfil our duty to our local communities is for schools to be part of a thriving trust. It's up to us to describe what a thriving trust is, using our own language, and we are well on the way to doing this.

We do know, as part of this, that a trust where the CEO, the Chair and the board work in unity is much more likely to thrive, so let us all take an oral workout and commit to gu-ber-na'to-ri-al (guː.bən.əˈtɔː.ri.əl) excellence.

WINNING MOVES

∞ Have a frank conversation early on in your relationship with the Chair of the Board and agree 'terms of engagement'. A verbal or written 'contract' capturing how you will work together. Before you agree, be clear in your own mind what will work for you and what won't. It might be regular and informal 'catch ups' outside of Board meetings or less frequent, more formal, structured one to ones. It has to work for both parties so be prepared to compromise to a workable arrangement. Remember how important trust is in the relationship and that this comes from transparency, honesty and open mindedness. Welcome challenge and adopt a 'no surprises' policy offering proactive assurance rather than reactive reassurance.

∞ View the Board and its members as a resource to be utilised as well as a body to hold you to account. Outside of Board meetings, get to know the individual specialisms of Board members and call upon them to add value to the key decisions you make and the major strategies you settle upon. Think about collective efficacy and be willing to learn from other sectors. Abandon ego and defensiveness and be 'one' of the experts around the table, not the expert.

∞ Exploit the potential of 'governance at point of contact' to keep you informed about the grass roots level impact of your decisions. See engagement at this level as a tool not a chore and use it to ensure you understand, first hand, how well the organisation is serving its key stakeholders. Get involved, on occasion, in each layer of governance from a 'listen and learn' perspective but don't interfere in due process.

4

Going for Growth

'Big organisations and small organisations are very different beasts and what will be expected and required of you as CEO will differ accordingly. It's best to know this from the start.'

In this chapter, Sir Steve considers the role of the Chief Executive and how it must adapt to the size, scale and complexity of the particular organisation. It explores how those growing their organisations must be intentional in doing so, mindful of the opportunities and challenges of growth, and how, as CEOs, we should be careful to ground the quest for growth not in a 'growth for growth's sake' mentality, but in a theory of the case for securing organisational sustainability and extending our reach so that more people can benefit from it.

Wrapped up in this is how a Chief Executive's role relates to, and contributes to, a scalable model of improvement. Sir Steve considers this and builds upon some of thinking in the fourth dimension of the Being the CEO framework - enabling improvement at scale. If, as is the case for many CEOs and organisations, we intend for improvement to remain an organisational habit as we grow to scale, we must be mindful about how we adapt.

We must consider how we can continue to ensure improvement continues to be generated across multiple sites, wider geographical distances, and through more agents operating at greater distance from the centre.

This is not an easy task - it requires a shift in approach from that of being the CEO of a small organisation; but getting this right can readily define the tenure of a CEO leading at scale.

****

We probably all have those series on TV that we get addicted to and watch avidly, even going as far as sometimes scheduling our social life around the day and time of its screening. I've had several over the years. One such series was Sex in the City. I loved the way that, at the start of the show, Carrie Bradshaw posed a question whilst writing her column and the way that the question was answered, one way or another, in the comedic, sad, ironic stories and screen action that followed. There was always a resolution and answer of some description, and I was hooked. I find myself in a similar position to Carrie right now, ready to pose exactly the same question that she did in one of those episodes. 'Does size matter?'

We are, of course, talking about completely different things. To find out what Carrie was talking about, watch the episode. My question relates to the seeming obsession in the academy trust world with the size of our organisations. 'How big will the trust be?' was one of the first questions I was always asked in the early days of being the CEO. How many schools? How many pupils? How many staff? It always puzzled me as to why it was such an important question to people. Similarly, it seemed to me to be the wrong question. Why this obsession with size? Surely you want to know what the organisation can do for you, how it will support and challenge you, how it will help you improve pupil outcomes, improve the provision in your school, what part you will play in the organisation and how you fit into the grand scheme of things. All these seemed to me more vital than just 'how big?

However, it seems that this is an ongoing issue because I'm often still asked the question by many Chief Executives in the position of seeking to grow their organisations. My first response is to meet a question with a question, 'why?' (a la Simon Sinek). Why do you want to grow the organisation? Why do you want to be bigger? I'm usually met with a range of responses. Some of which, in my view, are more convincing than others.

The answer with most fidelity, I believe, balances moral imperative with capability and capacity. The board and the CEO recognises that the organisation *can* do more and therefore *should* do more. The driver is what brought us all into education in the first place, improving the life chances of young people and giving them the best possible educational experience. The important bit here of course is this word 'can'. What do I mean by this? In the best possible scenario, I mean that the trust has an established way of continuously improving and sustaining the improvement of schools and has a track record that demonstrates this.

In addition, they have sufficient resources and capacity to ensure that they can successfully continue doing what they are doing with existing schools and use their spare resources and capacity to be doing the same with new schools. There is a bit more to it though, too. Before committing these extra resources elsewhere, the trust, I think, needs to be satisfied that in all major aspects, what it is currently doing for the children, staff and families it serves is of sufficiently high quality. A recognition that there is an opportunity cost to committing and investing precious resources to growth, and there are occasions when they might be better spent internally if something is not as effective as it needs to be.

This 'can and should' of course, is an ideal scenario and I acknowledge that getting a trust to this point is not easy and takes time. Many of the trusts I work with are nowhere near this point yet, but it's good to know what to aim for. For those trusts that are in this situation though, I have my own question, (which I used to a Board of Trustees I was advising who were too risk averse to grow, it almost got me thrown out!) How do you sleep at night knowing you could help more pupils and school communities and yet you won't?

I do recognise that this is the best driver and argument for bigger is better and this 'nirvana', as I say above, often seems illusive. The reality is that there are other drivers or imperatives that means trusts both need and want to get bigger and waiting for the perfect scenario described above is often not an option.

Let's start with 'need' and the principle of optimal size. If we were in the commercial business sector we would at least have a formula or well-established principle to help us. Try this one for size (pun intended):

'The optimum size of a business unit refers to such a unit that has all the factors of production in an ideal proportion such that, the factors of production are united in such a manner that maximum production is achieved at minimum cost. In other words, the profit earning capacity of a business unit is directly affected by its size. Therefore, the size of a unit should not be too big or too small. It should be of such a size, at which maximum production can be achieved, at minimum cost.'

Maximum production at minimum cost. Should not be too big or too small. Great.

Whilst I offer that to raise a smile, it's pretty clear to me that there are optimal sizes for trusts, but unlike the Department for Education or some other bodies, I don't settle on an ideal model or size or number. Note my use of plural – sizes. It's probably true, either extreme of size can be made to work with the right leadership, ethos and approach. I also categorically do not say that bigger is better. What a lot of nonsense the figure of 'at least ten schools' was in the largely abandoned 2022 White Paper. I can think of no rationale for that number. Doesn't fit with spans of control theory, (not a particularly important concept for me), doesn't take into consideration types of schools, different funding levels, different sizes of the business units.

It's always dodgy, as per my previous comments, to talk about the number of schools. Number of pupils is still a crude but probably better yardstick but there are so many other factors to take into consideration that it's a mistake to try and put a number on it. I get cross about this because there is so little 'learned wisdom' in our relatively immature academy sector about what constitutes optimal size, there has been insufficient research to draw meaningful conclusions and so, the DfE trying to steer to a place where they know, through inexperience, many will follow to an unsubstantiated indicative target is foolhardy. Leave it to those who have lived it and are actively living it now to use their wisdom to decide the right way forwards.

With that tirade over, I think there is one emerging 'truth' and that is, there is probably a *minimum* optimal size, again not a number, where a trust is big enough to enjoy the benefits of being bigger and yet small enough to retain all that is attractive about remaining small and trusts seeking to grow to this minimum optimal size is another of those arguments that, I think, successfully answers the 'why?' question.

I keep referring to the relative 'benefits' of different scale for organisations, so let's delve a little deeper into this because if we did a straw poll I think we'd probably find an even split in those who think that on one hand, "bigger is better" and on the other those who maintain "small is beautiful."

If you are in the first camp there are several factors which you would probably point to as being the significant benefits. The first of course, and the one that has been used most to support the policy of the growth of trusts, is the economies of scale that could be available. I say 'could be' because I'm not sure that if we looked closely at the actual practices of trusts at the moment, we would see that full advantage is being taken of this principle. How many trusts, for example, are actually GAG pooling? Many are not because of the internal politics around this.

The principle holds though, and we could argue that those economies of benefits traditionally associated with large scale do apply to MATs; specialisation and division of labour (experts that work across the piece and give access to the specialism that, perhaps, would not otherwise be available), lower resource cost through joint procurement and bulk buying, marketing economies of scale (national adverts for multiple purposes), spreading of overheads (one of those not two of those kind of principle), access to other streams of funding, (e.g. SCA), infrastructure investment (Technology) and so on.

This is just one side of the economies of scale argument, of course, because if we were to delve into diseconomies of scale that undoubtedly exist we might not be so convinced. One area that often gets scrutiny is the management costs of trusts. I read on Twitter at the weekend an analysis of MATs v LAs in terms of staff with salaries of £130000+. The largest trusts are, apparently, spending eight times more per pupil on salaries than England's largest LAs. Not the place to get into a debate on this but it's relevant to the (dis)economies of scale in trusts issue.

Other arguments in favour of the 'bigger is better' view centre on the ability of larger organisations to ride out tough times because of the levels of funding they attract and the reserves they are able to accrue, and their ability to invest in research and development as a result of the same principle. There's an argument, too, that larger organisations can attract the best talent because of the higher salaries they can offer. On the 'softer' side, in industry it's called brand recognition, and there are tangible benefits to this including being able to bring influence and, at its best, engender loyalty to the brand and attract customers. All of these may be the benefits of larger scale, it's a long list, but for me the issue is not whether they exist, it's whether they are utilised and maximised.

However, compelling an argument for bigger is better, the evangelists for keeping it small have some pretty good points too.
One of the most powerful being the ability to offer a custom approach, to take the time to get to know those they serve exceedingly well, to evaluate their needs and develop a solution that is perfect for them. They can become the definition of specialist. There are some brilliant examples in the academy trust world of small trusts who do exactly this, especially in the area of SEND.

There is potentially more flexibility, creativity and less bureaucracy in smaller organisations. Larger organisations tend to focus on consistency (I can't count how many thousands of times I've used this particular word as CEO) and process. Decisions can take a long time in hierarchical structures; smaller flatter ones can be nimble and responsive. I used to use the phrase 'turning the tanker' for major policy shifts, not such an issue at an organisation of a smaller scale.
I've chosen the word 'connection' to describe the next potential benefit. Smaller organisations have the ability to foster deep and meaningful professional relationships in a way that is very difficult when there are thousands of people employed. This connection can do so many things, it can provide a greater level of care for individuals, it can foster greater levels of engagement by making people feel part of the decision-making process, it can bring that 'family feel' that can be so attractive to potential employees and 'customers' alike.

I could go on, but I've hopefully made the point that there are pros and cons to both sides of this particular argument and it's not just a case of go big or stay small, of course, because it's all relative and there are stages in between, but 'how big?' is a question all CEOs have to answer. If this is the case, where to settle?

My advice is to find the right size for your why

In this instance, the why? is the legacy question I often ask people to think about. What does success look like to you when you step away? Which appeals to you more, 'big and bold' or 'small and beautiful'?

There is no right or wrong answer, you can be big and beautiful and small and bold, there is only a personal answer. One important consideration though is that big and small organisations are very different beasts and what will be expected and required of you as CEO will differ accordingly. It's best to know this from the start.

If your choice is to remain a smaller, nimble organisation then often you can rely more on the close professional relationships that you will have, close geography that makes practical things a bit easier and 'walking the halls'. It's probably true that the 'intentionally designed' culture of your organisation will be easier to sustain because of your closer involvement and because there will be less variables. In smaller organisations, CEOs can often quickly, personally, identify whether progress and impact is happening because they are much closer to the chalk face, in our case literally.

However, get beyond a handful of sites and into the realms of a larger cluster then it becomes a completely new ball game and CEOs will need to create 'organisational habits' - culture and practices that are generated, sustained and reinforced through systems and ways of working.

This is where the principles at the heart of the *seven pillars of improvement at scale* from Being the CEO are so helpful. In the book, Michael Pain provides a very clear and well-articulated model for improvement at scale and building, embedding and sustaining the various aspects of the model is key for the CEO and executive team.

The Seven Pillars of Improvement at Scale

1. **Having a clear narrative for what quality improvement looks like in practice**, linked to the trust's overall vision for education and learning (the importance of which we have already explored above).
2. **Having sufficient capacity and capability for improvement and innovation at scale**, recognising and understanding the role of 'leaders' of improvement at scale and 'deliverers' of it.
3. **Generating a culture of collective commitment across the organisation** to ensure the sharing of best practice, knowledge, resources and support for improvement.
4. **Generating systems that provide robust and real time data and intelligence**, that is timely, relevant and formative.
5. **Ensuring robust processes and project management** to ensure that improvement activity is timely, well planned, managed, and well understood by all.
6. **Ensuring that the organisation continues to invest in and encourage disciplined innovation**, and research and development, that is aligned with the vision and narrative for quality improvement, and that the organisation continues to remain at the cutting edge.
7. **Having a clear and robust quality assurance approach** in place that continuously monitors and reflects upon the impact of the improvement model itself.

Michael Pain 2019

The model covers those areas you'd expect to see when thinking about improvement at scale, such as constantly articulating and championing what is meant by quality improvement and success, ensuring the organisation has sufficient capacity and expertise at all levels to sustain and deliver improvement and, not least, investing in the talent, resources, and relationships across the organisation to support this. I like the emphasis that is placed on generating a culture of collective commitment to improvement across sites. We'll come on to our old friend Drucker and his breakfast in the next chapter.

If I summarise the various other aspects that make up Michael's model, it is clear that this offers a 'playbook' of sorts for those leading improvement at scale (whether that be in the 'big and bold' or 'small and beautiful' context). Ensuring the organisation has the systems and processes generating, accessing and responding to the right data and intelligence to inform continuous improvement; ensuring project management systems are in place across the organisation, and that these are well-managed and accessible to all who need it; and ensuring the organisation is able to constantly quality assure its work and the impact of the model, building in practices such as peer to peer review and external challenge - you pretty much get a handbook 101 of improvement at scale. And much better articulated than I could. Phew!

Within all of this, lies the difference between leading a smaller organisation and a larger or growing one, which is why I say it's a personal choice and, because the role of CEO is so different according to the size of the organisation, it's best to know from the start what you want to be doing with your time (and, crucially, what the board expects of you!).

Given the size of the trust I led, I'm often asked about the practical application of all this and how to build and operate such that improvement occurs and is sustained with a large and growing number of schools, children, staff etc. My answer is directly related to the observations I've shared above, and it is no coincidence that earlier, I asserted that it is possible to be big and beautiful because that is exactly the strategy I adopted as CEO. To build a big/small hybrid organisation that combined the benefits of both big and small companies.

I took my thinking from companies that had done a similar thing at an international and national level. Over the last thirty years many 'big' organisations have decentralised and established smaller companies under the umbrella of a parent company which oversees their work. These parent companies have the organisational resources and reach and influence of a big company but secure operational responsiveness and flexibility through the smaller companies. Intelligent organisational design. I thought my first attempt at this was the answer to this big/small hybrid. I established the trust as an umbrella trust responsible for ten smaller multi academy trusts each with their own articles of association but controlled by the Members and Executives of the umbrella organisation and operating under a scheme of delegation.

These smaller trusts were each responsible for a number of schools according to geography and we began building the 'small organisation' characteristics of these organisations and it worked well for the first year. Until the ESFA decided this was illegal (despite the DfE approving it) because of intercompany related party interests and ordering us to disband the whole structure and merge all eleven MATs. (I struck a deal to get that funded and out of the press!) Back to square one, after a few sleepless nights. But in fact it wasn't, because I realised that it wasn't the legal structures that mattered but the organisational and operational structures that would deliver the hybrid I wanted and so we moved to a cluster model, the rest as they say is history. By viewing these 'clusters' as in effect, small organisations in their own right and allowing them the degree of freedom and agreeing the parameters for doing this, we can capture many of the benefits of small-scale organisations whilst still realising the benefits of being part of a bigger whole. The cluster approach, which was innovative ten years ago is, I'm pleased to say, fairly well established now, using it to full advantage is the next challenge.

Let me finish by sharing a couple of principles on what, I believe, works best to secure this ideal hybrid of big and small benefits within trusts.

Firstly, a guiding principle needs to be getting the balance right between autonomous decisions made at point of contact and those made at the centre. If one of the 'small size' benefits we are seeking to secure is responsiveness to those we serve, then those directly responsible for this need to be given the flexibility and mandate to do so. A perfect example of this is decisions around what educational provision in individual schools and clusters look like. A one size fits all cookie cutter approach determined at the centre is unlikely to meet the needs of the very different communities that big organisations often serve, children in Croydon need a very different curriculum to those in Clacton for example. Let those who know those communities and their needs best, make these kinds of decisions.

Secondly, I think it's important to get the internal organisational structures right so that there is less hierarchy. A feature of large organisations is vertical and horizontal complexity which can lead to a sense of formal control. In any cluster or 'small company' model there needs to be flatter structures with decentralised decision making particularly at an executive and governance level. Giving thought of how the company organogram facilitates this principle is important.

Finally, there's the role of the CEO in larger organisations. If one of the benefits of smaller organisations is connection and developing the sense of 'family', well this can only happen if people have the chance to talk to you, share their ideas with you and let you know how they are faring in their professional lives. People need to feel noticed and important. As CEO of a large trust, I always worked on the principle of visibility and accessibility, making this 'connection' a priority.

My personal preference was to do this in an informal way and as much as possible. Whatever the way, the important principle is the ability of the CEO to help people feel part of the whole, however big that is.

So yes, Carrie, size matters. But big and small can work equally well.

WINNING MOVES

∞ Think about 'rightsizing' so that any scaling up plans you create for your organisation are closely linked to the 'why' of what you do. Understand the benefits associated with organisations of different sizes and those features you want to develop. Remember this can come through organisational design so think carefully about the kind of structures you put in place to facilitate this. Use the guiding principle of decisions as close to the point of impact as possible.

∞ Develop your own strategy for 'connection' with those across the organisation. Think about both the formal and informal opportunities you can provide so that people connect on a personal and professional level. Remember people like informality and to know what kind of person you are. Make a point of knowing something about the people you are meeting so you can refer to it when talking and don't underestimate the power of the CEO 'noticing' people.

∞ Have a very deliberate approach to developing your model for improvement at scale, and ensure it is clear and well-articulated to all. Making sure that everyone understands the model and their place in it is key. It is your job as CEO to ensure the narrative for improvement is continuously championed and reinforced, and to ensure the capacity, resource and collective commitment is in place to achieve improvement at scale across sites. It is also important to make sure that the systems and process - such as that timely and relevant data used formatively, and effective project management are in place across the organisation, that innovation is disciplined, and quality assurance is embedded. The seven dimensions of improvement at scale set out in *Being the CEO* are a really useful set of principles to reflect upon and begin to build your model around.

5

Is Culture King?

'Strategy creates the rules for playing the game, but culture determines the way the game will be played.'

This blog was written shortly after Forum Strategy's annual CEO Conference in September 2022. It focuses on an area that falls under dimension three of the Being the CEO framework - the role of the CEO as chief talent officer and culture maker.

In the blog, Sir Steve considers the question of whether culture really does eat strategy for breakfast, or, indeed, vice versa. As you will read, it's not that simple, but culture is, he says, probably the most important factor in ensuring workplace satisfaction and retention amongst staff at all levels. He reflects deeply for the first time on why culture building made such a big difference to his own leadership as CEO over the previous decade. In doing so, he provides some 'winning moves' that other Chief Executives can adopt. Finally, he asks, 'can we measure culture? How do we know whether the culture we aspire to is becoming a reality in the day to day working lives of those at all levels of the organisation?'

***

Three recent events turned my thoughts to the subject of this month's blog. The first was Forum Strategy's fifth annual national CEO conference which I found really uplifting, the theme of 'hope' being well timed and well-pitched. There was just the right dose of realism about the complex issues facing us all and the right amount of optimism about our ability to meet these challenges. The range of speakers, the subjects they touched upon and the different organisations they lead started me thinking about how organisations in different sectors operate, what makes them different but also what connects them.

Three of the speakers referred to the *culture* of their organisations and how 'it' was an enabler for what they were trying to achieve, whether that be CEO of a multi-national charity such as Oxfam, CEO of one of the largest market research companies, Ipsos UK or CEO of an amazing charity, Save a Child, born out of the herculean efforts of an extraordinary person. It was from Kelly Beaver, from Ipsos UK & Ireland, that we heard the first direct reference to culture in her use of Peter Drucker's now famous quote 'Culture eats strategy for breakfast'.

The second event was a phone call last week with a close friend experiencing difficulties at work and needing a supportive ear and good advice. He works in a branch of a well-known chemist's chain and was describing to me some of the issues he is having with his line manager, some of the challenges of working with colleagues he feels undermine him and finally, that he dreads going to work and if he didn't need the paycheque, would get out at once. 'It's such a toxic culture, Steve,' he said, 'I need to find a new job'.

The third event involved words coming out of my own mouth. The TES (Times Education Supplement) interviewed me last week for an upcoming profile they are going to run, a kind of exit interview from the sector. It's a glance back at the academy trust sector that was and a look forward to what is coming, interlaced with personal anecdotes and stories. One of the questions was 'What makes REACh2 successful, what was the biggest thing you got right?' My answer to the second question came unequivocally and instinctively. 'I got the culture right' I said. In hindsight, I'm rather glad the journalist didn't ask me to elucidate or expand too much as I don't think I'd have been happy with my on-the-spot answer. Given that I'd said this with conviction though, and 'culture' had come up in two other contexts, it did prompt me to give it more serious thought. 'Does culture really eat strategy for breakfast?'

My not so profound conclusion is probably it's not an outright 'yes', because in a perfect scenario, culture and strategy should complement and nurture each other, I think, and organisational transformation, which is what we are often all about, probably occurs best when they are perfectly aligned. After all, Druker didn't say that strategy was not important, just that in a game of Top Trumps (remember those cards? I loved that game) culture holds the winning hand.

As I pondered this and the three events noted above, a few questions sprung to mind. Firstly, do the three CEOs, the ex-CEO, and my friend all mean the same thing when they refer to culture (remember we are talking workplace culture here) and is there a working definition to give us all a common language?

Turns out you can get very hifalutin about it ('organisational culture includes an organisation's expectations, experiences, philosophy, as well as the values that guide member behaviour, and is expressed in member self-image, inner workings, interactions with the outside world, and future expectations' – thanks Forbes!) or you can go for a more narrative approach. My personal favourite, and the one I always use when talking about culture, goes something like; 'the shared beliefs, values and assumptions held by members of an organisation, visible in the way work gets done, evident in the language and behaviours of individuals and groups, amplified by the behaviour of leaders.' I say 'something like' because I can't remember if it's a definition or an interpretation someone shared with me. Whichever, it has all the elements (beliefs, values, language, behaviours) that I personally think make up the culture of an organisation and it was these elements that I focussed on when developing culture as a CEO.

Whilst I've been doing some reading on it, however, I've come across a couple of simple analogies that I really like. The first refers to the strategy vs. culture question and says that strategy creates the rules for playing the game, but culture determines the way the game will be played and, my absolute favourite, culture is an organisation's personality. And as we know with personalities, they can be strong, they can be weak, we can like them, even love them or, we can want to get as far away from them as we possibly can. As an interlude to sharing my thoughts on this topic I will, if I may, and along the way, give little provocations as to what you might like to consider about this question of culture in your own roles as CEOs. I do this because, in the mentoring I'm doing, it's a recurring topic of interest and I'm asked a lot about it.

So, to this end, my first provocation would be: Are you clear about what culture means to you and is there a shared understanding of this across your organisation?

So, let's get to it, why is culture so important? What leads Drucker to say it eats strategy and me to say it's at the heart of any success we had at REAch2? Well, as we all know, Drucker would argue that no matter how strong your strategic plan is, when it comes down to it, the people implementing the plan are the ones that make all the difference. His view: the efficacy of a strategy will be held back by people in the organisation if the right culture doesn't exist. If people in the organisation aren't passionate about the vision, they won't be enthusiastic about executing the plan, and the strategy stands no chance. Agreed. How many times in our early leadership careers did we write a policy, devise a plan, set up a process and be surprised when it wasn't successful or didn't work because, well, we are in charge, and it just should 'happen', shouldn't it? We learnt of course that's not how it works.

But it's not this deficit model of things won't work, happen or get delivered without the right culture that made building the right culture my number one priority as CEO, just the opposite, it was my conviction that *when the culture is right the true potential of the organisation can be realised.*

There are many reasons, in my experience, why this is true. Let me share just two.

Firstly, a strong culture helps people believe in the organisation, and this fosters commitment. For those within, a strong culture, where stated values are lived, not only builds a personal connection, but it also fosters trust. With this trust comes confidence and, I believe, greater engagement with the work of the organisation.

A positive culture is more motivational; people work harder because they believe there is purpose to their work. They are signed up to a clearly articulated vision and know that their contribution is valued. I have so many examples over the years where people have gone to extraordinary lengths to deliver on our work, examples of remarkable discretionary effort all because they *believe* in the organisation and know that their efforts are noticed and matter. This high degree of engagement makes us more effective. Put simply, culture impacts our performance.

Secondly, in a sector that is all about people, the right culture makes the organisation a place where people want to be. There are two aspects to this I think – it makes people want to stay, and it encourages people to join.

Most research into people management shows that companies that promote a sense of community in the workplace are more likely to retain their best employees – a workplace culture focused on people has profound appeal. On the other hand, the same research shows people who are great at their jobs and know the value of their skills commonly leave negative work environments where they feel undermined and unappreciated.

Back to my friend who wants to get out of the chemist shop because it is toxic. Throughout my own career, I've experienced both these situations and it was never aspects such as pay, conditions, workload that was the determiner in 'should I stay, or should I go?'. It was how I was made to feel.

So back to why culture was my number one success. Easy – because of it, we retained our best people, and we were able to attract top talent. People wanted to be part of the family. Culture is sometimes seen as something soft and squidgy and the term 'family' a bit twee. I've never been embarrassed to use it because it is a term that is associated with care, compassion, wellbeing, advice, guidance, responsibility, and even on occasion tough love. All the things that a brother or sister might want and need, all the things a colleague might want and need. All the things I might want and need.

There is a huge list of other benefits to an organisation that a positive culture brings; the way it can define your internal and external identity (and your USP), the positive impact it has on peoples' wellbeing, the way it makes people your biggest advocates (or critics remember!) and others. I've focused on just two. My provocation this time: Given its importance, are you paying sufficient attention to the culture of your organisation? Where is it on your list of priorities?

During the part of the TES interview where I said getting the culture right was my greatest success, Dan, the very affable journalist, asked a quite simple question which made me pause, because despite the simplicity of the question, I wasn't entirely sure of the answer. 'And how did you do it?' he asked. Good question.

I've given it some thought subsequently and have settled on three 'winning moves'. (A phrase we use a lot when we want to exemplify things that work). I'll share them in the hope that they will be useful.

Take time to nurture your culture – strong culture comes from intentionality

Firstly, because of good advice from the Chair of the Board, who had set up and run several successful organisations, I understood early on that *positive culture does not emerge organically, it is designed, constructed, and built with intent.* The Chief Executive's intent.

The truth is culture will develop with or without you. The difference is, without actively developing and shaping your organisational culture, you risk having all the negative flip sides of the positives I outlined above, poor engagement, unsupportive environment, lack of motivation and trust and so on.

So winning move number one, *take time to nurture your culture – strong culture comes from intentionality.* And start early. Culture reinforces itself and becomes more rigid over time so it's important to nudge it in the right direction as early as possible.

So, if a strong culture is designed with intent, what should we focus on?

Know what kind of culture you're intending to create

I focussed on three aspects, and then on my role in directing, nurturing, fostering and protecting each of them. The golden thread of the first two aspects leads to winning move number two, *know what kind of culture you are intending to create.*

For me, this comes down to values and beliefs, to who we are as an organisation and how we want to operate. The Touchstones, which have been at the heart of REAch2 for ten years, are an expression of the Trust's values; integrity, respect, responsibility, inclusion etc. We chose the analogy carefully – 500 years ago a touchstone was used to test the quality of gold, the deeper the mark in the stone, the higher the quality of the gold. For me, the deeper values are entrenched in our culture the purer we are.

The same principle applies to our beliefs. We built REAch2 on three simple beliefs which were turned into mantras – collaboration not competition, consistency not conformity, individuality not homogeny.

But what does this have to do with culture? Simple. This IS our culture and so determines our actions, our behaviours, our language, our decision making, our policies – everything. I once had quite a cheeky conversation with Lord Agnew who asked me what REAch2 was all about. I gave him the values and beliefs and said, 'you tell me'. We got on quite well after that.

Be explicit about the types of behaviours that are conducive to the culture you are seeking to establish

The next aspect really is crucial because it shows people how to be in the organisation. It involves peoples' behaviour and actions and their language. In some ways, of course, this is reliant on how much people are signed up to the values and beliefs of the organisation; the greater the alignment the more professional and personal behaviours will correlate with these. However, I've learned that this shouldn't be left to chance, and winning move number three is: *be explicit about the types of behaviours that are conducive to the culture you are seeking to establish.* Show people what is desired and expected. Validate the behaviours when you see them and challenge them when they fall short, including your own.

I don't want to teach you to suck eggs on this one, so I'll just share one example of something that really worked well for me. In trying to influence the behaviours of people in the organisation, my default position is always to start with the leaders. Over the course of a year, we developed, with headteachers across the Trust, what we call Leadership Propositions (ten of them). These proportions make explicit

63

what great leadership looks like within our Trust and what the associated behaviours look like. They are our leadership bible. We made sure that these propositions reinforced the cultural expectations and norms important to us. A few examples: leadership is about collective capacity, not personal status; leadership is about relationships; the primary focus of leadership is learning.

On face value these do let everyone know what we think great leadership is, but crucially important, great leadership within the culture of our organisation. The very people who are responsible for developing culture in all our schools have co-created some of the behaviours that go with it. We have made them culture advocates. One example of how you develop culture at scale.

Back to these provocations I like so much. Is culture something you are actively constructing in your Trust? And (sorry Peter Drucker) do you have a strategy for it?

Finally, a question I'm often asked about culture is 'how do you know if you've got it right? Can culture be measured? Safe to say that there is huge debate on this, and part of this debate is not whether it can be measured, but whether it should be measured at all. I certainly have my own view on this and an approach that worked for me. I'll share that a little later.

Firmly in the 'should be measured' camp is again our old friend Drucker (though this next quote is misattributed to him), 'what gets measured, gets managed', thus the argument that if culture is so crucial, then it needs to be managed. No argument from me on this.

The second half of this particular school of thought though is: if it needs to be managed, then it needs to be measured. Quite a lot of argument from me on this. Some people are still very firmly in this camp though and there has been a huge increase in the last decade of organisations identifying 'culture metrics' or 'culture indicators' and associated processes and systems to measure these.

To be honest, most of these indicators are unobjectionable. My meta-analysis of company culture metrics (who am I kidding? I looked at the websites of some big companies!) produced some areas of commonality centring on communication, innovation, agility, wellbeing, collaboration, support, mission and value alignment, performance. As constituent parts of a positive culture, you can't really object too much to these, a couple of them make it into the Touchstones I mentioned earlier. The big question for me though is do the sum of the parts make the whole? Can you reduce something as complex as 'culture' to a set of measurable metrics?

Those on the other (and probably my) side of the measurement argument would say no you can't and, anyway, not all that matters can be measured. They would argue that culture is so multifaceted and, because of the difficulty of precisely specifying the outcome we truly seek, should not be attempted. The fear being that easy-to-measure metrics would drive out the more difficult ones (can you measure such things as commitment, empathy, support?) and leaders would start off trying to manage what they want, and finish wanting what they could measure.

It's a fascinating debate. I've found my middle ground though and, as you'd expect, it's a compromise. There are some metrics that can help build up a picture of how strong your culture is. It does say something to know how many people are staying, leaving, joining the Trust, you can use surveys to find out how people are feeling. You can, if you are so inclined, use the formal constructs out there (someone once tried to sell me (unsuccessfully) the Organisational Culture Assessment Instrument).

I'm a simple man, however, and like simple solutions, therefore, when it comes to measuring culture, I tend to just watch and listen.

So, as I finish up, let me just end with a final thought...and an invitation. Developing and maintaining a positive, effective work culture is hard work, rooted in conscious effort and continued focus, particularly so during challenging times like those we are all experiencing now. I have shared my perspective with you here but wouldn't it be fascinating to take this further and share thoughts and experiences across the wider national CEO network? I look forward to continuing the conversation with all of you on this hugely important topic.

WINNING MOVES

∞ Recognise that culture is constructed and be intentional in its design. Think about core culture (what sits at the heart of the organisation - vision and values), emotional culture (what it feels like to be part of the organisation) and operational culture (how business gets done). Consider using a culture design template or canvas (Razetti's is a good one) and treat it like the implementation of any other major strategy that needs embedding and sustaining across the organisation.

∞ Identify 'cultural ambassadors', those people best placed to transmit cultural pollen across the organisation. Consider those people whose role intersects and interacts with key stakeholders. Spend quality time with them to develop them as role models of the behaviours, attitudes and language you want to foster. Develop 'cultural indicators' to exemplify to everyone what your desired culture looks like in practice.

∞ Take a regular litmus test. Develop both formal and informal ways of testing out for yourself how well the desired culture is becoming embedded. Walk out informally across the organisation and have a 'public opinion shower', letting people's words and behaviours rain down on you, and listen and reflect. Identify your own 'litmus people', those people who without fear or favour will tell you as it is so that you can take action if necessary.

6

The Power of Networks

'A great peer network can help solve problems, can identify practical solutions suitable for all, and can generate ideas about different ways of doing the same job. It's a learning opportunity.'

In this blog, Sir Steve reflects on the importance of networking, and ongoing learning and development generally, in the role of Chief Executive. He admits early on that 'it is lonely at the top' and writes on how it is almost impossible for CEOs to have a truly unguarded, frank relationship with those they lead. 'You're the boss' he writes, and sometimes you can't or shouldn't share your worries or concerns internally.

So, where do CEOs turn? Well, for Sir Steve it's to mentors and coaches, and to carefully selected leadership development networks that exist for Chief Executives. The former is a professional, confidential relationship where we can be at our most vulnerable and open - which often leads to the greatest gains; the latter brings a sense of community, of solidarity, and an opportunity to stay focused on the bigger picture and learn from the experience of others. Sir Steve reflects at length on the characteristics of impactful networks for CEOs.

****

I was reminded by Forum Strategy's CEO network event this week just how important connection is. "It's lonely at the top" is a cliché that has been bandied around for years, yet it is still a feeling many of us

67

have today. Harvard Business Review reported only this year that half of all CEOs they surveyed expressed feelings of loneliness and, of these, 61% said this loneliness hinders their performance. This sense of loneliness, isolation, detachment – call it what you will – is especially true, I think, for new CEOS who suddenly realise that the type of relationships that they had prior to taking up the role, even if it is in the same organisation, no longer exist in the same way and need to be redefined. It's a similarly tough challenge for an incoming CEO, no matter how experienced, because the stripes are not yet earned, and people's trust is not given lightly. And even for experienced CEOs, and those long in the tooth like me, there's always that knowledge that you can't (and shouldn't) have that completely unreserved, unguarded, 100% frank relationship with those you employ or line manage. You're the boss and you're paid to keep some things to yourself and (maybe) some secrets. No point in turning to the Chair of the Board or other Trustees either. They are your boss.

Whilst I'm a big believer in transparency and honesty, it's just plain politic to have that professional, frank, constructive relationship with those who govern you rather than a warts and all, "I'm on my knees, I can't cope, give me a hug" kind of relationship. But let's be clear, there will no doubt be those times when the latter is exactly what you need, (because we are going for those Bold Ambitions, right?) So, where do you look? Most of us probably default to loved ones at home or friends which, whilst very comforting, is probably not fair and, from bitter experience, doesn't always turn out well. Loved ones and friends can empathise, console and encourage but very rarely can they completely understand and help you solve whatever problem or issue is confronting you – because they are not doing the same job. (And even if by some chance they are, it might be like two tsunamis hitting each other). These long years of experience have taught me that better answers lay elsewhere. Two places in fact. In a professional mentor/coach and in a well selected peer network.

To briefly cover the first, that relationship, built over time and bound by confidentiality, is probably the best place to be at your most vulnerable, to be completely yourself and share those warts and all revelations. This coach/mentor can either be within the sector, or outside of it (I've experienced both and there are pros and cons to each) and can - bearing in mind their distinct roles - provide that listening ear, space and good reflective questions that move us along in our thinking (coaches) or shoulder, advice and guidance (mentors) when you need it. It's such a vital thing to have. But so is this well selected peer network I refer to because, although it's probably not going to give you the same degree of professional intimacy that a one-on-one relationship will, it's a good start in addressing this 'lonely at the top feeling', and more to the point, it can bring so much more in addition. What more?

Well firstly, it can bring a sense of belonging. A sense of community. Definitions of community include: 'a group of people sharing a particular characteristic (same job maybe?)' 'A body of people connected by certain attitudes and interests in common' (...for the purposes of education'). 'A group of people who want to achieve something together' (bold ambitions?). However you define it, you're not alone in it, and here's where being part of that well selected network starts to tackle the issue of isolation and loneliness.

But there's more, of course. At a recent Forum Strategy CEO network meeting, I talked about how, as a result of the experience of the pandemic, there has been a shift in how CEOs are behaving. One of those shifts is a willingness, desire, almost a need to collaborate with other CEOs. Why? Part of it is about commiserating each other on a really tough job and part of it is connecting with people facing the same leadership challenges. But a very big part of it is the realisation that a great peer network can help solve problems, can identify practical solutions suitable for all, and can generate ideas about different ways of doing the same job. It's a learning opportunity. And it's here, I believe, where such great value exists. Imagine a scenario where there is open source on the very best practice from some of the most effective organisations around. Who wouldn't learn from that? And who could resist such an opportunity?

As well as being great professional development, my own experience of being part of a peer network has brought other benefits too. It's helped me see the bigger picture. It's an all-consuming job as we know and it's easy to become insular and focussed on our own organisation and its challenges. Recognising that there are other challenges out there that peers are facing has helped me develop a more holistic view of the educational landscape and, more importantly, a better understanding of broader societal challenges. Working with cross-sector, cross-phase CEO peers, in different parts of the country, has deepened my understanding of the purpose of what we are all trying to achieve in quite a profound way.

Let me throw in a one liner that is equally as true as all the other reasons above. A well selected peer network brings fun, and on occasion, even joy, to what we do. A friendly word of encouragement, an amusing anecdote, even a bit of dark humour if the proverbial hits the fan, makes a world of difference. It shows empathy and solidarity. And we all need a bit of that.

Reader, you will have noticed that I keep overusing this phrase 'well selected'. It's not a stylistic fault, it's deliberate. There are several networks out there and choosing the right one to really invest in is crucial, and it depends on what you want to get from the network, and also, what you are prepared to give. Joining the Forum Strategy CEO network, originally as a member and ad-hoc contributor, and most recently in the privileged position of Chair of the CEO network, is me selecting well. Why? Firstly, I want to be part of a network that gets to know its members well, that is about striving to meet the needs of all its members and where all members, big or small, are equally important and valued. Equity. I've been part of networks where loud voices from big trusts drive the agenda, it's just not right. And I opt out.

Secondly, I want to be part of a peer network where collective success for all matters and where a culture of professional generosity, learning and sharing is encouraged and facilitated and where it can be done with a sense of optimism and fun. Again, that hasn't always been my experience. Finally, it's really quite important to me that any peer network I am involved in is independent, not reliant on quangos for funding and is most certainly not too aligned with government. This isn't a political comment in any way, or a criticism of any other network, but, having navigated nine changes of Secretary of State for Education (maybe ten by the time you read this) and ploughed my own path for ten years, one thing I'm certain of. It's far better to chase your dreams than our (temporary) political masters.

One of the things I always struggled with a bit as a CEO was how much I should use my voice as a leader of a large trust to comment upon issues both within and outside education and how political I should be. Whether my job was to solely focus on the job at hand, improving schools, giving children great life chances etc., or whether commenting on and getting involved in the broader societal issues came within my remit. In industry terms the former is called shareholder value theory and the idea is that, in that arena, CEOs are qualified to make profits not lead society. That thinking has moved on quite a lot in recent years and we see that most large corporations now have a commitment to social responsibility and some high-profile CEOs are being called CEO activists, that is using their privileged position to influence policymakers and law makers on things which matter to them both as an organisation and, often, as an individual.

Most commentators say this is now being driven by a number of factors. Firstly, the workforce is changing and 'millennials' (and those coming after) are much more likely to focus on an organisations impact on society at large and the environment and to insist that, if they are to become part of that organisation, it has a strong social mission.

Certainly, over the last few years, I've been asked much more frequently and passionately about this by people applying to work at REAch2. Secondly, globally, there seems to be declining confidence on the part of executives, and many others, that governments will step in and fix some of our biggest problem; from sustainability to social mobility, and inequality. Add onto this our other challenges of a cost-of-living crisis, war, political turmoil etc. and we start to ask the question, well who is going to sort all this out?

I read a startling fact recently (it was in Forbes so I'll give it some credence); 70% of the largest entities on earth are corporations not countries. Think about that. If that is not a mandate for CEOs to be societal leaders, I'm not sure what would be. I'm not, of course, suggesting that as trust CEOs we have the scale to be that influential but we are a small part of it and the principle holds. Because we have a social responsibility to the many, many thousands of children and young people in our care, we have a duty, I would argue, to get involved in wider societal issues, a duty to speak out and a duty to act, even if government can't and won't. That sounds like I'm calling for a revolution and of course I'm not, but I feel really strongly that we should do what we can. So, what is that?

Firstly, we can convene voices and we can influence. The education system is fragmented, we all know that. Even within our own peer network we will all have slightly different agendas and priorities but there are some universal truths and experiences we are all living through that unite us to some common ground, values and issues. Equality, equity, social justice, sustainability. We need to explore as individuals and as a peer network what these really mean to us, what change we want to see and then we need to make our voice heard. The sector and society at large needs it.

Secondly, we can champion and advocate. I was really struck by how passionately Jayne spoke at our recent network event about protecting the needs of vulnerable families and children with SEND, and really understanding the scale and size of 'the tiger' we are grappling with as we go forward in this area. Multiply the passion, determination and resolve of Jayne to make a difference and advocate for these families by the number of CEOs in our network and I would suggest that's a force to be reckoned with and has the potential to make a huge difference.

Thirdly, we can be what I call a 'societal litmus'. I made a reference at the network event to a shift I was seeing on Twitter and other social media whereby high-profile figures in our sector have been calling out the government on issues of ethics and morality. This is heartening. Civic leaders holding to a moral compass and challenging when the high standards we expect are not adhered to. It's not just about politicians though, but everyone who holds a position of authority and responsibility to others, including Trust leaders. Understanding our collective responsibility to be active and not passive in creating a fairer more equitable sector and society is something we can all do.

Finally, we can make sure that we are as responsive as we possibly can be to those we serve. Finding out what matters most to our children and families and doing what will make the most positive difference to them needs to be number one on our list of priorities. Societal leaders respond to other people's agendas, not their own. The process of talking to all our stakeholders to find out what they wanted from our organisation was the biggest eye opener for me at REACh2 last year. Three of the top five priorities were not even on my list. It's why I urged those of you in the session this week to make sure you are fully connected with your families. It was heartening to see how many CEOs are doing this right now. Let's encourage everyone to do the same.

To finish, I'd like to signpost to the National #TrustLeaders CEO conference, which has taken place every September since 2018. It's an event I'm really looking forward to again this year because it's a theme dear to my heart. Hope. It's not often listed as a leadership trait, but it ought to be. In a recent blog I started to touch on this and referenced that hope is about painting a picture of a better future, it's about pursuing what ought to be. I signalled that in this complex, VUCA world we find ourselves, bringing hope is one of the most important things a CEO can do. I'd like to link this with the thought I shared at the network event this week, that 'being' as a CEO is as important as 'doing', because after the session I started to wonder what 'being' hopeful looks like. I've settled on a few things for now.

Firstly, I think it's about being eternally optimistic, glass half full, silver lining and all that. Hopeful leaders, I think, believe tomorrow holds greater opportunities for personal and organisational success. They are forward-thinking, inspiring, enthusiastic and relentlessly positive. Secondly, hopeful leaders focus on the best in people, not the worst. Celebrating the success of people in their teams, their unique talents and not over dwelling or being too harsh about any failures. Hopeful leaders embrace failure, recognising that failure is rarely final or fatal. In fact, it's required. A bold vision means courage is paramount and a mindset that asks, 'what did we learn from the mistake in the last venture that will now get us to the next level?' There's something also, I think, about how hopeful leaders are self-motivated, with their vision and ambition being intrinsic so they don't need a mandate or permission to follow it, but I want to give that one some more thought.

Hope is not, of course, a guarantee for success, but a great leader, I believe, will take the slightest amount of hope and use it to chip away at the barriers of reality and impossibility.

WINNING MOVES

∞ Build your resilience and fortitude in being the CEO by investing in a high-quality coach and mentor. Recognise that it can be a lonely job so find that person who can sustain you on a personal level during tough times. Understand also that you need to be challenged on a professional level to become a better CEO; find a person who can do both. Think creatively and move out of your comfort zone by finding someone out of sector or someone who has a different career history, a more senior job, is more experienced so that you develop more diverse perspectives. Realise that this is a long-term investment in yourself and should only stop when you do.

∞ Spend time in building a powerful peer network and leverage what that brings to you and the organisation. Ensure that you engage with a network that is about collective success, embraces collaboration as well as competition and where there is sufficient synergy in your values to make collective advocacy a possibility. Remember the opportunity costs in investing time and energy in networks that add little value and avoid them.

∞ Embrace the opportunity to make a difference not only to the individual communities you serve but more broadly to society at large. Identify what role you want to play as a societal leader and build your influence in these areas. Be clear which of the 'big issues' matter most to you and commit your organisation and yourself to supporting that agenda and becoming an expert authority on it. Choose carefully the forums to express your views on these topics.

7

Risk-taking and an Investor Mindset

'People who don't take risks generally make about two big mistakes a year. People who do take risks generally make about two big mistakes a year.' (Peter Drucker)

In this blog, written in April 2023, Sir Steve builds on the theme of dimension five of the Being the CEO framework - leading organisational sustainability and compliance. In it, he goes to the heart of the question around how much risk is too much risk and how do we manage it? In doing so he admits that managing risk was his steepest learning curve, but one that - ultimately - he got right where some of his contemporaries sadly failed.

What made the difference? 'My thinking shifted', he writes 'from believing that risk is something that is all about keeping us safe, to seeing it as something that allows us to know our organisation better so that we can do more.' He goes on to consider the concept of 'risk universe' that helped him throughout his tenure, and the important distinction between risk tolerance and risk appetite.

Related to all this, and building on the theme of dimension five, Sir Steve goes on to consider the role of Chief Executive as investor. Investors, he says, see the budget as the beginning, looking at not only how they can spend it efficiently but also invest it wisely. They are thoughtful, deliberate and take a long view in relation to organisational design and capacity building, looking for wider sources of funding and income generation, investing in people and delivery models that are more efficient, and looking outwards to make connections. They see the budget as the servant of the organisation.

Finally, Sir Steve returns to the themes of dimension three, and the role of CEOs as Chief Talent Officers. He considers the partnership with and role of the Chief Operating Officer and writes at length about the role of CEO as investor in people. CEOs, he writes, 'consciously construct a culture that 'looks after' their most precious asset including their health and wellbeing.'

****

When asked ten years ago about my ambitions as a CEO for the size and scope of the trust I was establishing, I was unequivocal in my response and it went something like, 'not sure of the details but a national academy trust, fifty plus schools and all over the country. Primary only'. That was about as sophisticated as my growth strategy was at that time. It was premised on three things really; ambition (to do more for the types of school communities I loved working with), a mental model of how it might work and, in hindsight, a spectacular disregard for the degree of risk I was taking in pursuing such a venture. In the history of the growth of the trust, the founder school was in East London, the first sponsored school in Hertfordshire and the third school, a successful bid to open a brand-new school, in Staffordshire. At the interview for that project the Department for Education academy broker asserted, 'I know you will have detailed plans for how you will make this work, Steve'. 'Yes', I responded and offered no detail. Because there was no detail.

It was at that point that I knew it was going to be a national trust, because now it had to be with the geography already spanning 135 miles.

The rest is history of course, but as I reflect on that moment in time, I recognise a couple of things in myself that have been a constant feature of both my personal and professional life. I'm a risk taker and

I have an entrepreneurial spirit. These two things have led me down a couple of paths common sense says I shouldn't have followed, and not to the end I necessarily desired, but there is no doubt they have also been central to any degree of success I have had as a CEO and so I'd like to spend a little time on these subjects if I may in the hope that it will be of interest and helpful.

Understanding risk probably represents my greatest area of learning as a CEO and like so many aspects in my professional learning, came from engaging with an expert in another sector, a Trustee working in international banking.

Through this tutelage I came to understand that risk, correctly defined, approached and managed, is a fundamental business concept that can make a huge difference to how businesses and organisations are run. All organisations have to take some risks and avoid others, of course, and to do so, they need to be clear about what successful performance looks like. But this learning shifted my thinking from believing that risk is something that is all about keeping us safe, to seeing it as something that allows us to know our organisation better so that we can do more. It can release our potential.

There are certain phrases associated with risk that are now part of my everyday vernacular, and thus that of the organisation, but the starting point was much more basic than this. It was to understand what risk actually is because it soon became evident that I was mixing up two things: risks and issues. I now define risk as an event or outcome which could happen and, if it did, would have an adverse impact. This impact may affect a person (child or adult), a group of people, a school or its community. Equally, the impact may affect more than one school, or a function within the trust, or indeed have a trust wide impact. By definition however, if a risk has materialised then it is no longer a risk, but instead is now an issue which requires action locally or by central teams and/or Executives.

The example I use when training people (yes, I've become a bit of a risk nerd) comes from one of our schools where hypodermic needles were being found in the playground and thus entered on the school's risk register. But, of course, the needles aren't the risk here, they are the issue because they are already in the playground, the risk is someone picks them up and comes to harm as a result of them being there. A simple but important distinction. Important because it meant that those hundreds of colour coded boxes on spreadsheets at school and trust level (sound familiar?) weren't identifying risks but issues. Oops.

The first thing I learnt to do, therefore, was to properly define what we (and the Institute of Risk Management) call the *Risk Universe,* that is all the actual (known) risks that the organisation might face.

Now, as a trust we identified just eight at school level (yep eight, not dozens and dozens), and all subsequent processes and procedures for risk management were built around these eight areas. Let me share them with you and, in the spirit of playful provocation, challenge you to find a risk that doesn't fit into one of these descriptors.

Risk one is all about Health and Safety as you would expect. Here's the descriptor. There is a risk that a child, member of staff, or a member of the public comes to actual physical harm, due to either an unsafe condition or systemic failure to manage health, safety and property related risks. This could result in: Death or serious injury with potential for civil litigation; Failure to comply with statutory duties with potential for prosecution; Cause serious property damage or render an area unsafe for occupation.

Risk two focuses on Safeguarding. There is a risk that a child or children comes to harm as a result of abuse or neglect. This could result in: Serious harm to individuals; Legal action against the trust with potentially significant financial implications; and External intervention affecting outcomes for others.

Risk three is about Quality of education. There is a risk that school leaders are not ensuring that the school provides an acceptable standard of education. This could result in: Onerous and increased scrutiny which stretches trust resources; Declining numbers of pupils; Damage to staff wellbeing. Reputational damage; Adverse external inspection outcomes; and External intervention – DfE re-brokerage.

Risk four focuses on Personal Development, Behaviour, and Attitudes and adds: Declining numbers of pupils; Damage to staff wellbeing to the adverse effects listed under Risk three above.

Risk five is concerned with People. There is a risk that the trust is not able to deliver its goals because of a lack of capacity / capability across schools due to: the loss of key talent; failure to recruit to key posts or underperformance due to a lack of key skills or poor staff engagement / wellbeing. This could result in: Damage to the Trust's ability to deliver its goals; Adverse impact on wellbeing of other staff; and Increased likelihood across other risks.

Risk six is about Finances. There is a risk that a school and/or the trust fails to meet its financial commitments as a result of, for example, financial mismanagement, low pupil numbers or unforeseen costs. This could result in: Damage to the Trust's ability to deliver its goals; Closure of the Trust or financial penalties; and External intervention – DfE re-brokerage.

Risk seven is Operational. There is a risk that a school and/or the trust may encounter loss due to operational failure as a result of, for example, IT system failure, communication failure, project delivery failure or key supplier failure. This could result in: Damage to the Trust's ability to deliver its goals; and Increased likelihood across other risks.

Finally, Risk eight is about Legal and Regulatory Requirements. There is a risk that the trust fails to meet regulatory or legal obligations (e.g., data held by the trust is breached or lost). This could result in: Financial penalties; Diversion of management and executive focus to address the issue and its consequences; and reputational damage.

I don't usually share such detail in my blogs, but I do this time as this literally transformed the way in which we looked at risk and moved the organisation from a tick box culture to one where there was a mature, rounded conversation about *strategic* risk which became a living, breathing process rather than just a set of identification or measurement activities at any one given time. (There are a corresponding set of descriptors at a whole trust level focusing on groups of schools should anyone wish to see them).

All this detail about identifying risks properly is leading somewhere (phew!) and that is, if we believe, as I do, that no organisation, whether in the private, public or third sector can achieve its objectives without taking risk, the really important question is how much risk should they take?

To answer this question, I think CEOs need to be really assured and have a clear understanding of two things. Firstly, the organisation's *Risk Tolerance* and secondly its *Risk Appetite* and each of these need to be built upon an accurate assessment of how much exposure currently exists in the risk universe. (Hence the importance of the above).

I always think of Risk Tolerance as the risk we can just about get away with and Risk Appetite as those new risks we want to engage with to further advance the objectives of the trust. Almost two sides of the same coin; taking risk as well as exercising control, pursuing risk whilst understanding what we can deal with. Most risk management experts would recommend that Risk Appetite should be developed in the context of an organisation's risk management capability, which is a function of risk capacity and risk management maturity.

In the example above, in the early days of my CEO career, there was plenty of Risk Appetite, but much less understanding of the trust's tolerance for risk. Dangerous territory. And so, I'd like to emphasise the important link that, I believe, exists between a clear and accurate understanding of an organisation's Risk Tolerance and a CEO's ability to be *safely* entrepreneurial in pursuing their Risk Appetite. It's an area that I feel is often undervalued by CEOs and wrongly delegated to others (often the COO). I believe CEOs should make all things risk their number one priority and see it as the enabler that it is.

CEO as Investor in Chief

Let's, with your indulgence, use the above as a context setting to an aspect that I want to move on to, and that is the principle of the CEO as Investor in Chief. The context is relevant because in this aspect of their role the CEO is operating in two of the eight risk domains, finance and people, and the judgements, decisions and actions which they take should, in my view, be heavily influenced by their understanding of their organisation's tolerance for risk.

Michael Pain focuses on this brilliantly in 'Being the CEO' (both within the book and the programme) and makes the important distinction between CEOs as bean counters or as investors. I don't want to repeat his work so will just remind us that, for Michael, investors see the budget as the beginning, looking at not only how they can spend it efficiently but also invest it wisely, that investors look for wider sources of funding, and income generation, invest in people and delivery models that are more efficient, look outwards to make connections and see the budget as the servant of the organisation.

I wholeheartedly agree with these and would add (or rather emphasise) a couple more.

For me, Investor CEOs focus on the long term and are sometimes willing to make sacrifices in the short term. They think in terms of five to ten years rather than simply in terms of one or two, and they are concerned with enduring impact and legacy. I was reminded of this idea of enduring impact and legacy at the weekend in Barcelona when I visited the stunning Sagrada Familia designed by Gaudi. It was, of course, the awesome beauty of the church that took my breath away, but I was equally struck by the fact that Gaudi knew he would not live to see the completion of his vision, believing that it would take 200 years (we only sign a lease on schools for 125 years!) but that his contribution to it would lay the path for others to follow and it was investment in something extraordinarily beautiful for the future. There's an analogy for you. (When asked about this, I like his rather droll 'the patron of this project is not in a hurry').

In addition to this long-term view, Investor CEOs are, I think, able to accurately forecast sector or industry changes and adapt accordingly, and, to my mind most importantly, they understand that their greatest resource is their people, and spend their time in personally nurturing, developing and harnessing their potential and talent.

To offer a few reflections on this topic. I think this is all about mindset. Investor CEOs have a mindset that sees resource allocation as a strategic move both on its own and as an essential enabler of other strategic moves. They are open-minded about resource allocation and, indeed, re-allocation. They believe that it's not about constantly generating income and resources but sometimes about using existing resources differently. Research shows that companies that re-allocate more than 50 percent of their capital expenditure over a ten-year period create 50 percent more value than companies that are slow to do this. We might argue that in our sector 'value' is hard to define, but the principle holds. The same research shows that a third of companies reallocate just 1 percent of their capital in this period. I suspect that this is the case for many organisations in our academy trust world as we tend to default to historical spending models and incremental change. In my view, as CEOs we need to be more ambitious in ensuring that resources are swiftly allocated to where they will deliver most value rather than being preoccupied in ensuring they are spread thinly or equally across all operations, we need to make more comparisons using appropriate metrics to prompt us when to stop funding something and when to continue it.

Furthermore, I think Investor CEOs think a lot about organisational design. And about the agility and the responsiveness of their organisations. They think about how they are structured and how they operate. There was a paradigm shift in our working practices during the pandemic and this has shown us that we can do things in a different way. There's an argument to be made that CEOs should now be determining which features of their organisational design will be stable and unchanging (e.g., permanent roles, signature processes) to deliver core purpose and which will be dynamic, responding to changing demands and new challenges (temporary teams, flexible sourcing). It's a contentious thought, but it's also a mindset.

One from Michael's list that I touch on elsewhere, so won't repeat at length is that Investor CEOs understand the value of strategic partnerships, networks, alliances and know that engaging with the external environment, the meaningful outside, is ultimately a vehicle for operational and organisational growth.

On a personal level, one thing that allowed me to be an Investor in Chief was forging probably the strongest professional relationship I had, and that was with the trust's Chief Financial Officer, who became the COO. This was particularly important for me for two reasons. Firstly, the importance I allocate to managing finances is underdeveloped. (I was often in debt with big overdrafts as a student and young teacher resulting in my bank manager (a friend of my dad's) reminding me, 'Steve, you do actually bank with us and not the other way round) and secondly, in balancing my own risk appetite with the CFO's thoroughly grounded understanding of the trust's financial risk tolerance. The traditional view of the CFO, that of the bean-counter;

risk averse, eyes firmly in the spreadsheet, perhaps not seeing the bigger picture, couldn't be further from the truth in this instance and the analogy she used with me was that whilst I owned the terrain, she owned the map, and she was 'the enabler' in our professional relationship. Again, that all-important investor mindset.

Before I move onto a final reflection about the CEO as Chief Investor in People, let's be clear, all organisations do need to use resources as efficiently as possible, avoid waste and prioritise what matters. It's not an either/or, there does need to be a deal of bean counting alongside the investment. Thorndike's work on the most successful CEOs of the late 20th Century reminded us that nearly all of them worked out of bare bones central offices and spent little on 'flashy' promotional gimmickry or image. It's why I would never invest in central offices for the trust, for example, or spend a lot on brochures and magazines. CEO investors spend their money wisely according to their priorities and understand that lean is mean. I love the quote attributed to Bill Hewlett, co-founder of Hewlett Packard, who observed: 'More companies die of indigestion than starvation'.

To finish, three reflections I'd like to make on this 'mindset' of the CEO as Investor in Chief, and these relate to people within their organisation.

Firstly, investor CEOs want maximum return from their investment in people and so they manage performance and wellbeing with equal rigour. There is general acceptance in financial portfolio companies that they would rather put money on an average strategy in the hands of great talent than on a great strategy in the hands of average talent. We are not in that sector, but the principle holds. I think Investor CEOs think systematically about their people, which roles they play, what they can achieve and how the organisation should operate to increase people's impact. On one hand this looks like moving swiftly on under performance, not leaving inadequate performers in key positions so that the potential of the role remains unfulfilled and zero tolerance on attitudes and behaviours that cut across the culture of the organisation or impede the mission.

Equally, however, Investor CEOs ensure the organisation goes beyond a 'normal' employee value proposition and offers gold standard learning and development opportunities, carefully manages and tracks the progression and career of the most talented employees and rigorously measures and manages all cultural elements that drive performance. They consciously construct a culture that 'looks after' their most precious asset including their health and wellbeing.

Secondly, and perhaps unsurprisingly, CEOs of this mindset align value and talent. They have a healthy disregard for positional authority within their own organisation and ask the question; 'Who has the best qualities to lead this?' rather than 'Whose job is it?' and in seeking to maximise value they are much less concerned with positional authority and more with collective capacity. As a CEO, I used to think about the 'availability of leadership' across the trust rather than roles and responsibilities.

As an aside, when it comes to talent management, Investor CEOs are much more likely to appoint and promote on potential than on anything else. They will happily ignore inexperience, for example, with the belief that, with the appropriate investment, the reward will be greater.

Finally, CEOs as Investor in Chief see themselves as one of the organisation's most valuable assets, which is not about ego, but a recognition that they themselves are a resource to be invested and will apply their time, energy and effort to what brings most value. For me, it was always people.

Let's end a blog on this theme with wise words from someone who really understands the principles behind all of it. I've admired the career of Mellody Hobson for quite a while. She is currently Chairwoman of Starbucks (the first black woman to be chair of a top 500 company) and before that, one of my favourite film production companies, DreamWorks. I agree with her in asserting; 'The biggest risk of all, is not taking one'.

WINNING MOVES

∞ View risk management as an enabler of bold moves and a culture maker for entrepreneurship. Play an active role in shaping the organisation's approach to risk and grow to understand its tolerance for risk. Learn to align your own appetite for risk to this tolerance.

∞ Recognise that people are your greatest asset and invest in them as much as possible, expect exceptional return for this investment in terms of performance, attitude and commitment. Look after people's wellbeing to the best of your ability. View yourself as a resource to be invested and dedicate significant time and energy in personally nurturing potential at every level.

∞ See investment of organisational resources as a test of character and strive to get comfortable with feeling uncomfortable. Aim to strike a balance between prudent conservation of resources in the short term and a willingness to be patient and invest for long term gains. Regularly scan the horizon for opportunities and be decisive when a good one presents itself.

8

No More Islands Anymore

'It is about cultivating partnerships that help us to deliver our mission more effectively.'

In this blog, written in November 2022, Sir Steve reflects upon the theme of dimension six of the Being the CEO framework, the role of the CEO in fostering key external relationships and building social and professional capital in doing so.

He begins by considering the day-to-day work of CEOs, and his regular challenge to those he is mentoring around whether they are spending sufficient amounts of their time on 'CEO type things'. One often underestimated activity that falls into this category is that of spending time fostering strategic partnerships that bring vital social and professional capital to the organisation. This requires us to engage with complexity and people to a degree that is not required in other roles. It is a defining part of the job.

Sir Steve considers the importance, especially for senior public sector leaders, of engaging with politicians and civil servants and shares his 'Goldilocks' approach that has served him well over the years. He also reflects on the growing importance of community engagement and ensuring that CEOs and their organisations are genuinely connected to their local communities and work in partnership with them.

****

When it comes to leadership, we all have bees in our bonnet about certain things. Mine is making sure that what we do as a CEO matches our pay grade and the responsibilities bestowed upon us as leaders at this level, including trying to meet the expectations (quite rightly) staff and communities have of someone operating at this level. It's something that I constantly ask those I'm mentoring for Forum Strategy and beyond, to reflect upon. It's not an arrogant 'those types of tasks are below us' kind of thing, more a recognition that as the most senior executive in an organisation we should be doing those things that add the most value, that make the most difference, and that deliver more bang for the bucks.

It was John West Burnham who first helped me explore this and, in our coaching sessions when I first became CEO, encouraged me to focus much more on the strategic aspects of the role and to 'do' a lot less operational type activity. To lead more, manage less, and administrate as little as possible. We developed a neat little matrix to help me consolidate my understanding of this and to use with other leaders in the organisation to exemplify what we meant. This was twelve years ago but I still swear by it today.

We based this matrix on the principle that there is a continuum. At one end of this continuum sits 'leadership', at the other end 'administration', and in the middle, 'management'. Thereby defining the type of activities that we can spend our time on.

We exemplified these activities by thinking about the *principle* of each, the *purpose* of each and how this related to *people*. As I have set out in an earlier chapter, the principle that sits behind leadership is doing the right things, the purpose is path making and with people, it is engaging with the complexity of any given situation. In management, the principle is doing things right, the purpose is to follow the path and for people, we seek to create clarity. At the far right of the continuum, administration, the principle and purpose is simply doing things and path tidying and with people, it is about securing consistency. We didn't make this a hierarchy or use a pyramid model, preferring a continuum, in recognition that at times all of these are valid activities that those in leadership positions do. We did, however, and I still do, maintain that the more time we spend on 'leadership' type activities, the more we sit at the left of the continuum, doing the right thing, finding the path, engaging with people and complexity, the more likely we are to be effective in the roles we hold. The more likely we are to add value to our organisation, to help it fulfil its mission and achieve its vision.

One of the things I sometimes ask CEOs to do (you might like to get a pen and paper and try this) is to reflect on the type of activities that they have undertaken, in the last week, month etc. and categorise them in accordance with the above, to get a picture of where they are currently sitting on the continuum. The answers are often surprising and remind us how easy it is to become consumed with managing and (ouch!) administrating and not making time and space to get out of the weeds, onto the balcony and actually lead.

As I (nicely) challenge people on this issue, the question I often get is, 'what is a leadership type activity as a CEO'? What should I be spending my time doing then? I'm going to use this blog to give one example: engaging with the complexity of the external environment.

I do believe that for many of us with an educational leadership background (still the vast majority of trust CEOs, but it is changing) becoming and being the CEO in our sector is a challenging leadership transition. Whilst the path to this role has prepared us reasonably well for key internal leadership responsibilities (such as building and leading executive teams, crafting vision and strategy etc.) many of us have far less experience managing the external environment: working closely (or not) with government and its agencies and (mostly!) civil servants, the political arena of maverick and oft changing ministers and MPs, the (to be feared or courted?) media and other key external stakeholders. The varying demands can be overwhelming and, I believe, CEOs can be at risk of falling into some classic traps. I did.

One trap is not spending enough time managing external relationships. It's so easy to focus on what we know, and where we feel comfortable, running the trust. This is especially true if there are significant operational issues that consume our time. The dangers of underinvesting in external engagement can rapidly come home to roost though if there is trouble on the horizon but, more to the point, a chief executive who has cultivated authentic relationships with the communities, agencies, and people outside the organisation will begin to build capital, capital that can be put to good use. More on that later.

At the opposite end of the time-allocation spectrum, there are CEOs who get too caught up in the swirl of external activity and don't spend enough time leading their trust. It can be completely appropriate for a CEO to focus much of his or her time externally, but only if it adds value to the organisation and only if there is a strong team (and, potentially, a capable leader, such as a Chief Operating Officer) running internal operations. Even then, a CEO can underestimate the degree to which their time and attention makes a difference internally. Ultimately, there is no substitute for CEOs when it comes to articulating vision and strategy to their organisation or communicating the rationale for change.

A subtler trap, I think – one I've seen far too much of – is spending too much time on activities that advance a CEOs own interests or image, and not enough on what really creates value for the organisation. As CEOs, we typically have many opportunities to participate in forums, events etc. and speak to interesting audiences; it's all too easy to be pulled in and become distracted by all the attention. That's not to say that CEOs should ignore their passions or personal brands; a strong public profile can of course create value, but I would humbly suggest, if you find yourself spending a considerable amount of time engaged in external activities that are stimulating and self-affirming but remain of questionable value to your organisation, it's time to step back, reassess and reset.

So how do we avoid these traps and ensure that engagement with the outside world does what it needs to? What helped me was being clear about the purpose of any such engagement, and that purpose was to shape the external environment to further the trust's mission and help me to refine and deliver upon our strategy. This might seem obvious, but the right framing can bring clarity to what we should and shouldn't be doing and it can help ensure we allocate time and energy to the types of engagement that add most value, and that generate the capital we need to deliver this mission. I always try to remember the opportunity costs of such endeavours and that whilst I'm 'out and about' my attention and focus is not fully on the organisation itself, so there's a careful balance to be struck.

'Capital' will vary from trust to trust depending on the mission but there are probably some common themes. The positives are about enhancing the reputation of the trust, identifying possible opportunities for development and growth, creating partnerships that bring knowledge and new ideas to the organisation, generating capacity, bringing influence to bear on policy makers and so on. On the other hand, of course, there is building capital (metaphorically stashing money in the bank) for dealing with crises and emergent external threats or when the proverbial hits the fan (at some point in a long CEO career it probably will). So in such a complex and highly charged environment, who, why, when and how should we be engaging?

I've always taken a fairly pragmatic approach to this by categorising the external environment into groups, people and organisations I felt it was either: *necessary, desirable,* or *self-sustaining* to engage with.

Let's start with the latter. In an earlier article I hit on the loneliness of the long-distance CEO. Given the overwhelming responsibility and pressure on us to appear calm for those around us, to be the rock that the waves crash upon, to consistently deliver results and to be where the proverbial buck stops, it's no wonder that as CEOs we tend to isolate ourselves. This is not just an education sector issue; In a previous article I quoted the Harvard Business Review finding that the majority of cross-sector CEOs (61%) express feelings of loneliness and believe that this hinders their performance. It can be problematic to find the solution to this internally whether that is not wanting to worry those who work for you, not wanting to fully share your vulnerabilities with those you work for and, to be honest, there is only one CEO of your organisation and it's you so no one can fully empathise.

My answer to this is to look externally. I found what I called my 'true north group' of peers; three fellow CEOs who were in a similar position to me, weren't afraid to give some tough love and honest feedback, could help me keep perspective in tricky times, but also helped me develop a sense of belonging and of professional community. It's a two-way process, of course. At various times we act as nurturer, grounding rod, truth teller, and mirror for each other. At other times we try to challenge or inspire and of course, sometimes, we console and give a hug. But we are always there. This undoubtedly helped me through the vagaries of life as a CEO, helped sustain me, and in terms of capital, was well worth the time I invested in it. No surprise we are still close friends even though I'm no longer in the role.

One of the strengths of a leader, I believe, is knowing what you don't know and when I was thinking about setting up the trust twelve years ago, I realised that I didn't know or really understand the context in which I would be operating. The academies movement was relatively new, and it was unclear to me how schools joined trusts, who made the decisions, and how it all worked. Given I knew I wanted to build a large organisation, I thought I'd better find out. Like any good MBA graduate, I defaulted to an organisational developmental model and did my PESTLE. It didn't take Einstein to realise that this was and still is a highly political environment. Of which I had zero experience. In setting about rectifying this the stars aligned, and I was offered a job at the DfE in the very department responsible for academies and trusts and I became (on secondment) a sponsor development adviser and sponsor broker. Very handy. It is here that I learned how it all works, further strengthened by a three-year stint on a Headteacher Advisory Board. (Some might call this being opportunistic, I prefer 'scanning the horizon and putting my PESTLE to good use').

I have some wonderful stories about the brokerage of certain schools to certain trusts which I am not a liberty to talk about and wouldn't want to because it wouldn't paint a great picture of what 'the wild west' looked like in the early days. It's better now. But still not good enough. Where I am going with this is that in my *necessary* group sits all things political. That includes the DfE, Regional Directors and their offices and officers, the ESFA, politicians, ministers – that bunch.

It would be naïve to think that we are not operating in a political environment. I know you know it because so many of you talk to me about your frustrations with it. CEOs often feel ill used by the current system or believe that they can use the system to their advantage if they form the right relationships with the 'right' people. Some believe there are 'favoured' organisations and feel overlooked, some people struggle to see the rationale behind decisions coming out of some of these offices, others bemoan the lack of transparency. Most say, where is the consistency? There are elements of truth in all of this. Believe me.

But much as Gandalf (you know I like my literary allusions) replies to Frodo's:

"I wish it need not have happened in my time,"

"So do I, and so do all who live to see such times. But that is not for them to decide. All we have to decide is what to do with the time that is given us."

And so, it is for us, all we have to decide is how to engage with this. For engage we must.

A CEO analogy I like is that of the 'Business Diplomat' because diplomats reflexively think politically. Just as diplomats seek to advance the interests of their nations, as CEOs we need to engage with these powerful external players to advance the interests of our organisations and create value for all parties. And herein lies the rub. These political masters have their own agenda, want their own pound of flesh and we have to be a diplomat in the sense of listening to them, understanding what they want, and finding a way to deliver it. The real skill is in doing this in a way that aligns with what we want. Some of you might rail against this and think it's a political game. Yep, that's right. Let me give you an example.

Growth was on my agenda pretty much most of the time I was a CEO, in the early days sometimes the answer was yes, sometimes it was no. I learned to get a yes by understanding the problems and the issues the Regional Schools Commissioners had to resolve. Can't get sponsors in that part of the country? No problem: if it's a cluster of six schools we will go. Worked several times. Now of course that's a fairly extreme example and not everyone is in a position to deliver on that, but the principle holds. Understanding the political agenda of our gatekeepers and engaging with them in finding this out is something that will bring capital to us.

In less specific terms I'm often asked about 'how' to manage this relationship with the politicians and civil servants. I always advocate 'The Goldilocks approach' which is about ensuring the amount, type, and detail of communication you have with them maximises the chances of success in what you are seeking from them. Getting it 'just about right'. In terms of 'too cold', if there is no engagement or very little with them then the trust won't be on the radar, and this is ok if there's nothing you want, not so good if you're seeking growth for example. In the 'too hot' category is over sharing. We all believe in transparency, but 'political transparency' is what I go for. A warts and all low down on your trust is probably not a great idea. Simply because that's probably time specific and things move on and inadvertently raising alarm bells can take a long time to dampen down. Let's be clear though, one thing that any politician or civil servant does not like is nasty surprises, just like the Chair of the Board, so my policy has always been if there is bad news on the horizon, flag it and discuss it and use the capital you hopefully have in the bank to offset it.

This final category, desirable, you might argue should be called essential because it is about cultivating partnerships that help us deliver our mission more effectively. It's about those connections that firmly root us in the heart of the communities we serve. I categorise this type of external engagement as desirable, because although it is crucial, it is not always easy to cultivate. All sorts of barriers exist to building and sustaining this type of connection.

The importance of this was brought home to me nearly twenty-three years ago. I was in my second headship on September 11th, 2001, when a teaching assistant ran in and told me of the terrible events. Like the rest of the world, we all watched in horror. The school is located right next to Finsbury Park Mosque (which at the time had its own issues of suspected radicalisation) and has a 60% Muslim population and it's safe to say that the tension within the school community was intense. Each morning for days afterwards in the playground I was playing peacemaker and appealing for calm. This could have ripped the school community apart. Instead, what happened was two leaders of neighbouring 'institutions' connected, recognised their duty to their shared local community and worked together to bring first calm and then over time, greater cohesion. It was this that first as a leader, demonstrated to me so clearly the power of local partnership and its potential to improve the lives of those in the community. More of this has got to be 'doing the right thing' I suggest and any links, relationships, partnerships of this nature that CEOs engage in, and which help social cohesion, should firmly be recognised as building capital.

There are so many more examples of how local partnerships can contribute to social mobility, social cohesion and can generate cultural capital and how this is central to a 'thriving trust', and therefore a crucial aspect of the external environment the CEO needs to engage with. Much of the work of Forum Strategy around academy trusts at the heart of their communities (with multiple case studies), and upcoming work on thriving trusts, will be a valuable source of ideas and inspiration for Chief Executives in this regard.

I'll finish with a gentle nudge to spend as much time as you can in doing 'CEO' type things, thinking of the principle and purpose of leadership and remembering that management is efficiency in climbing the ladder of success, leadership determines whether the ladder is leaning against the right wall. (Administration probably fills in the risk assessment).

WINNING MOVES

∞ Understand the 'why?' of engagement with the outside world, whether it is necessary, desirable or self-sustaining to engage with different bodies, organisations or people. Commit time and energy commensurate with the returns to the organisation and to yourself. Remember there is an internal, organisational 'opportunity cost' to outside engagement and carefully balance internal and external focus.

∞ Take time to fully understand the macro environment in which you operate, the 'meaningful outside'. Think particularly about the political, social and economic context and connect with those bodies, organisations and people who are the 'gatekeepers' within the sector you operate. Strive to be an active influencer. through your engagement with them

∞ Invest time in trying to secure one important partnership with a company or individual who wishes to invest in social capital. Focus on a relationship that will bring sustained and significant value. Identify the aspect of your 'USP' that is most likely to strike a chord with those wishing to invest, develop it into an attractive proposal and create a strong narrative to explain the additionality it will bring and the benefits to the 'investor.'

9

Ethics, Leadership and Anti-leadership

'We can learn from the very best and we can learn from the not so great. Just as long as we learn.'

One of the four foundations of the Being the CEO framework is ethics and standards. In 2022, the issue of ethical leadership came to the fore as a deep sense of controversy emerged around alleged breaches of COVID19 restrictions by then British Prime Minister, Boris Johnson. It was an issue that undermined his leadership and government, and ultimately led to his resignation in July that year.

In this blog, written a few months after Johnson's resignation, Sir Steve considers the lessons from a fundamental loss of trust in what he describes as the 'CEO of the land.' He also takes a step back to consider the tenure of Liz Truss, Johnson's immediate successor who herself resigned from office less than fifty days into the job. For Sir Steve, this example of 'anti-leadership' leans more to the second issue of standards. Truss, he concludes, failed to listen, to learn and to connect as she embarked upon her premiership and, in doing so, failed to make well-informed and advised decisions and stick with them. Instead, the focus appeared to be on what was politically expedient, and when it turned out it wasn't politically expedient, she 'u-turned' to try and make it so. Great CEOs, he reflects, seek out the contextual wisdom and ensure their leadership is grounded in the views, experiences and advice of a wide range of people, not what scores short-term points.

Behind so many failures of leadership, Sir Steve concludes, looms the influence of too great an ego. We're all in danger of it, and a CEO that aspires to lead congruently, and with sufficient humility and impact, will keep it in check. The ability to demonstrate strong ethics and high standards, as we will read, depends upon it.

****

John F Kennedy is often quoted on leadership, and of the many important things he said, one of my favourites is the quite simple but profound *'leadership and learning are indispensable to one another.'* A recognition that no matter how experienced a leader is, or how successful they might be, there's always room for improvement (at least, there is for those with humility, more on that later) and to strive for continuous refinement in our art form should be every leader's personal mantra.

Looking at the leadership styles and strategies of some of those considered the world's greatest leaders has always been a bit of a hobby of mine, if you're going to have a leadership lesson, it might as well be from the greatest, and a bit like Malvolio in Twelfth Night (though hopefully not as duped or vainglorious) have come to see that yes indeed, *"some are born great, some achieve greatness and some have greatness thrust upon 'em"*.

Of course, Shakespeare was writing in times of Kings and Queens, and a monarch was born 'great' because they were expected to become the leader of a country, and whether they were in fact, 'great 'leaders per se is open to interpretation and debate. You know my views on Queen Elizabeth II from an earlier blog. I'd probably add Queen Elizabeth I to my list of great monarchs too (interesting, both female); whether King Charles III reaches these dizzy heights is still to be seen.

But it's not those 'born' into greatness that I'm interested in right now, but those who achieved greatness through their efforts and/or talent. Many incontrovertible 'greats' fit the bill – Mozart, Galileo, Einstein,

(Debbie Harry) etc. but whilst they were leaders in their respective fields, it's not the type of leadership I'm focusing on. So, it is to the world of politics and the leadership of nations that I turn my attention to see what lessons in leadership can be garnered for trust leaders and the answer is, many great lessons of course. At the end of this particular article, I will share a couple of the lessons from just one (in my view) truly great leader, the one who has had the most impact on my thinking and approach even though he led hundreds of years ago.

BUT. How can I talk about lessons in leadership without looking at what is happening with the leaders of our own country of late? For those of you who know me, you know I largely remain apolitical, so this isn't about scoring cheap hits, it's about looking at those recently and currently in, arguably, the most senior leadership position (CEO of the land, if you will) and seeing what lessons in leadership there are. Correction. What lessons in anti-leadership there are.

Lessons in 'anti-leadership'

I'll keep my observations on the (anti) lessons provided by Liz Truss brief, commensurate with her time in office. Let's just say Shakespeare would have been proud of this tragicomedy/farce – 'Is this a lettuce I see before me?'

Michael Pain rightly talks with great clarity in his book *Being the CEO* about the need for contextual wisdom, the need for the CEO to interpret the 'meaningful outside' and to ensure this interpretation of context and climate is used to inform both a leadership narrative and leadership strategies. To use his analogy in the book, when there is a misalignment between what the 'farmer' is growing and selling and what the 'market' wants to buy then inevitably trouble lies ahead. And the market decides.

Let's take Liz Truss as an example here. A brief look at the 'meaningful outside' shows, of course, that Liz Truss took over at an exceedingly challenging time, with price rises adding to a cost-of-living crisis, her own political party almost at civil war, and a real war taking place in Ukraine. People were feeling overwhelmed and scared. They felt that tomorrow may well be worse than today. They needed hope in the new leadership.

The need to connect with those she was there to serve should have been overwhelming for Liz Truss and her strategy ought to have been clear (when rich oil companies shout 'tax us', you really should listen and not do the opposite). But instead, she made her fatal leadership mistake – she failed to listen, she failed to consult and, when she set about soothing peoples' worries by cutting taxes for the already rich, she failed to properly interpret the meaningful outside (and inside, given the reaction of many in her own party) and paid the price.

The absolute necessity of connecting, listening, understanding and being responsive to those we serve is a theme I return to often and once again I encourage us all as leaders to reflect upon how aligned our own priorities and strategies are to the things that are most important to those in our Trust and school communities. We will all have our own formal and informal ways of doing this. My favourite method was best described by Abraham Lincoln, a leader of a different calibre, who took regular walks out into towns and cities across America to experience 'public opinion showers'. A brilliant way of hearing first-hand how those we serve are being affected and are responding to our decisions and actions as leaders.

The second (anti) leadership lesson comes from what can only be described as the political whiplash and emotional turmoil brought about by an extraordinary set of u turns, enough to garner the title of 'flip-flop' prime minister. I'm always interested in this notion that a u turn is a bad thing; switching from a bad decision to a good one should be welcomed, surely? In the world of politics, of course, the issue is that politicians don't want to admit that they got anything wrong, or have changed their mind, as their opponents and others will make capital out of it, which makes the need for good decision making ever more important.

This rapid reversal in decisions we all witnessed sparked my interest in how good and bad decisions are made and what lessons there might be for those still making them. Some things are obvious; understanding the type of decision to be made, understanding the context of the decision, having sufficient information to take the decision, recognising your emotional state when making decisions etc. All these things are important. Similarly, we all have a natural decision-making style. There has been lots of research into this and by my favourite set of descriptors (Cheryl Einhorn) I would categorise myself as an *adventurer,* quick, trusting my own gut instincts, and unafraid to make decisions fast. There are other styles of course; the *detective* who is data and evidence hungry and believes more 'learned' equals better results, the *listener* who seeks input and opinion and takes comfort in not making decisions alone. The *thinker* who weighs options, makes reasoned decisions and for whom speed is secondary, and the *visionary* who seeks new and different things and likes to keep everyone guessing and surprised. There are pros and cons for each of these, of course, and the virtue of recognising your own natural resting state, combined with understanding what type of decision is to be made and the willingness and ability to bring in more of what is needed to move forward positively (whether it's diverse types of decision makers, thinking or simply sensitivity to time) is, I believe, at the heart of effective decision making.

I've casually said that understanding the type of decision to be made is really important too. I like the approach Jeff Bezos took at Amazon in categorising decisions. He had a two-type rule. Decisions that are irreversible and of consequence, which he called 'one-way door decisions' as you don't get to go back through if you change your mind. And reversible 'two-way door decisions' where you do. In his view, you don't want to make a one-way door decision quickly, they deserve a lot of thought, debate and consensus.

I can't help but wonder if Liz Truss got two things wrong here. Firstly, not recognising that she needed to make a fair few of what should have been one-way door decisions and didn't commit sufficient time and thought to this, and perhaps didn't pay enough attention to *how* the decisions were taken so they turned into two-way door decisions (u turns). Secondly, as I covered above, did this with insufficient clarity about the meaningful context she was working in.

One thing is clear, as Prime Minister, or CEO, you don't need to be right all of the time, you're not *the* expert, but (really) you do need to get things right most of the time, be *an* expert, if people are to have confidence in your judgement and ability, which is so crucial to trust and authenticity.

There are other lessons from this ex-Prime Ministers short tenure, (don't promise more than you can deliver, it's just as important to align your team behind an idea or a belief as it is to take the decisions necessary to implement it, listen to criticism, it will probably help you make better decisions) but for me these two are the biggest takeaways.

Where to begin with Boris Johnson?

This is a tricky one. There was much mirth and a little bemusement in our household last Christmas when a handwritten Number 10 Christmas card arrived, 'Steve, Christmas wishes, Boris and Carrie'. A little bit conspiracy theory spooked, 'where did they get the address?', a little bit 'how did I get on that list?' and a little bit (naively) 'aww he remembers!' Yes. I know (knew) Boris. There, it's out in the open. It's quite something in your first Headship to find out that one of the country's larger than life characters has put some of his (now grown up) children in your school, but so it was with Boris, who was then editor of the Spectator, and so it was for five years. One of the most difficult things I've had to personally reconcile is my experience of Boris as a parent and the public persona of the politician and former Prime Minister before us all.

It was an auspicious start, I persuaded him to host a PTA quiz and be the compere. I had written the questions and with his well-documented charisma, he held the room of parents and staff enthralled. He did, however, consume a number of bottles of beer and as the evening progressed kept mixing up which handheld the microphone and which the bottle of Becks – much to our delight, we often had to chorus 'Boris, use the other hand'. There's also the occasion that he was on Question Time and was asked if his children went to private school, to which he replied, 'Oh no, state school, run by a young trendy guy with an earring'. (Oh! to still be that) I'm not here to reminisce about that time but would like to say that I had nothing but good experiences with him as a very involved parent. Just a fact.

As a recent former Prime Minister, he is, however, going to contribute to an (anti) leadership lesson. It's a short and devastating one. Once you lose the *moral* authority to lead, *positional* authority is pretty meaningless, and you might as well pack your bags and leave. Which he did.

I know I'm on sensitive ground here because we will all have our own views, and I don't want to offend anyone. So let me tell you the

102

reasons why, *on a personal level,* I believe he lost his moral authority to lead and, to be clear, it wasn't just one event or issue that led me to this conclusion, more, *lingchi* – death by a thousand cuts, but it's all related to one factor – ego.

I really can't be doing with ego. It's dangerous. I know, I almost fell foul to it. In the early days of the academy movement there were some very big egos around and just like Boris quite a few of them came a cropper. My take is as we rise in the ranks and our 'power' grows we get in a 'bubble' where we start to be a victim of our own hubris, a victim of our own success and start to see the world differently, act and behave differently. Excessive ego, at its worst, warps perspective, twists values and corrupts behaviours. This is what I believe happened to Boris. Why do I say this?

Firstly, I believe a leader should be culpable for their own actions and honest in the face of mistakes or errors of judgement. An egotistical leader does not reflect on personal shortcomings because it would interfere with their need to feel superior. If we look at what happened over many, many months, after each of the government's PR disasters, (and there were many) a familiar routine occurred – apologies were made, excuses were formulated, and alibis were given. But not by Boris himself. Instead, we were faced with a roll-out of junior ministers to take the fall for whatever allegations the prime minister was facing at the time. No one finds it easy, (including me) to trust someone who, despite being completely found out, still tries to shift the blame elsewhere.

Secondly, with ego comes, I believe, a sense that the rules don't apply to us, that we are somehow above them, a sense of do as I say not as I do. Nothing was more shocking to me than the constant stream of images and stories about party gate at a time when the very great majority of us were doing the right thing and behaving in the way we were asked by our political CEO. In outlining, to me, the most important of the four foundations of the CEO role, that of values, ethics and standards, Michael asks us the question: '*are you ready to live and work in a way that is congruent with the standards of behaviour you and/or your Board expect of all those working within the organisation? Can you model this?*' Such an important question. Because if the answer is no, the consequences are huge. They were for Boris, and they will be for anyone who follows this anti leadership lesson. In my mind there is no way back once this 'reputation' is lost. Ask Othello, "Reputation, reputation, reputation! Oh, I have lost my reputation! I have lost the immortal part of myself, and what remains is bestial."

We're used to taking our cues and learning from leaders who we consider to be great, but the fact is, you can learn just as much from the leaders you come into contact with who are less-than-perfect, and if 'leadership and learning are indispensable to one another' then let's take every opportunity to learn that which is in front of us.

I very rarely focus on what could be called the negative. I did a talk on hopeful leadership at the Forum Strategy national #TrustLeaders CEO conference earlier this year (see Appendix 1) for goodness sake, so let's return, and finish on a more positive note.

All of us, I'm sure, have those 'greats' either in history, or more contemporary, who inspire us and from whom we take great learning. I count myself extraordinarily lucky to have come across mine. I was in Washington on a rainy-day one November many years ago and went to the Lincoln memorial, which in itself is an awe-inspiring monument. Fascinated by the detailed history and the portrayal of Abraham Lincoln's role as President in the American Civil War, reading about his leadership became a bit of an obsession for me. Many people have studied this leadership and written about it, and I've read quite a lot. At the heart of all of it though are some really simple lessons in how to lead, such common sense that the 'Lincoln's Principles', as they are called, have become my leadership bible. There are a fair few of them, hence all the study, but here are three to whet your appetite. (I take no credit for this meta-analysis, check out the brilliant work by Donald Phillips)

One I mentioned earlier. Taking public opinion showers, to secure that understanding of the meaningful context. 'Get out of the office and circulate among the troops', he advised. Use the opportunity of casual contact to get the most accurate and up to date information, to have casual conversations that will lead to commitment and loyalty, to give sincere praise when merited, to show that your people are your most valuable asset and to show that you are willing to do the things you ask people to do. A real understanding that when you get amongst people you create community, collaboration, and commitment. I interpreted this as be a visible, accessible leader, and be human, and

I always actively built-in time to do this, not leaving it to chance, though not missing the informal chance when it arose.

Another principle was to influence people through conversation, humour and storytelling and in doing so preach a vision and continually reaffirm it. His view was that people are really interested in stories, not facts and it's the stories that they will remember. His approach was to communicate with people like 'they are an old friend', talk to them without self-consciousness, superiority or pretension. In doing this, he advocated, embody the values you hold and the vision you wish to gain acceptance for. My favourite quote of his on this subject was along the lines of 'my vision is only as strong as the soldier posted in the furthest regiment from Washington can articulate.' Different context, same principle. True in 1861, true in 2022.

I guess my favourite of all is 'be a master of paradox'. There's so much leadership literature out there on this notion. The view being that leaders who are heavily biased toward one side of a paradox are less effective than leaders who can manage said paradox. The best leaders, it is argued, use both sides of the paradox to formulate balanced solutions to difficult problems. I agree! So, what paradoxes did Lincoln suggest we balance? Three of them. Be flexible, yet consistent, depending on the situation. Be trusting and compassionate, yet demanding and tough, and be a risk taker and innovative, yet patient and calculating. Whatever has been written since 1861, there's nothing more succinctly brilliant than this in my opinion.

How to conclude? Leadership and learning are indispensable to one another. JFK is right, of course. We can learn from the very best and we can learn from the not so great. Just as long as we learn.

WINNING MOVES

∞ Recognise that integrity is at the heart of every authentic leader. Be explicit in developing a moral framework, write down your beliefs, values and principles as a compass to guide your decisions and actions. Regularly reflect on these to ensure they stay strong. Create mental scenarios where your moral compass would be tested and rehearse your response in preparation for the real thing. When you encounter a lighthouse moment or crucible experience, reflect on your response and determine how satisfied you are with it and what you will do the same or differently the next time.

∞ Understand the importance of quality decision making. Restrict yourself to those decisions that significantly impact the business and delegate the rest to other people. Recognize that quality, timely decisions improve effectiveness. On irreversible decisions, triangulate with those around you with more expertise and try to achieve consensus. Come to know your own decision-making style and make an objective judgement on its appropriateness to the context of the decision to be taken.

∞ Avoid 'importantitis' and learn to keep your ego in check. Try to listen more than you speak, adopt a coaching rather than telling style and surround yourself with equally strong people who will keep you rooted in reality. Invite their help in avoiding hubris.

10

Me Being Me, You Being You

'The great thing is, as CEOs the power is in our hands to be able to do this for so many people, and we must make it our business to drive the changes needed.'

This final article of the book, written a few weeks before Christmas 2022, is probably Sir Steve's most personal so far. In it, he goes back to his roots and reflects on his upbringing, his family, and the reality of being gay, a son of a miner, and growing up on a tough estate in Sheffield in the 1970s.

Sir Steve reflects on his early professional experiences and how, in his words, they were characterised by fear of stigma, reluctance to talk about his personal life, dread that it would become an issue for his career progression and a general feeling of isolation. Building on the theme, Sir Steve reflects on other characteristics - such as age and gender - and how these, he suspects, had a bearing, positively and negatively on his career.

The chapter sets out how, as CEO, Sir Steve, though more than aware of the impact of discrimination and lack of inclusivity, also recognised he was not the expert in achieving equality, diversity and inclusion across his organisations. He sets out the thinking and some of the practices that inspired and drove change during his tenure as a Chief Executive, not least the importance of the board owning and modelling the equality, diversity and inclusions agenda.

This final chapter includes many important reflections and much important guidance, but probably most profound is Sir Steve's reflection on being open as a CEO about his sexuality, and the view, for those he leads that 'me being me, gives you the mandate for you to be you.'

****

Once upon a time in a land far away, Sheffield, lived a hardworking man who toiled long and hard every day under the earth, in search of that most precious of minerals, coal. The man lived a happy life with his wife who laboured equally hard in that most dangerous of occupations, dinner lady. Despite these humble circumstances they were happy because they felt blessed, blessed by having a family of two wonderful daughters and, at long last, after eight years of waiting, they had a baby son. The father was so happy that he finally had a son. He loved his daughters, of course, but now he had another man in the family, and could do all those things that fathers do with sons. He would teach him how to build things, he would play his beloved rugby with him, the boy would learn how to look after himself in their tough world and would be afraid of nothing. And the boy would have his own children and carry on the family line.

So ends the fairy tale. It wasn't very long, about seven years in fact, before the boy realised that when it came to the stories his mum used to read to him, it was Prince Charming that was by far the most interesting character to him. And though wearing Cinders' frocks, (be they tatty or ball gowns), held no interest, nor was there a desire to squeeze into a crystal shoe, being carried off into the sunset by a guy with muscles (and a brain of course) must be quite something.

That seven-year old's innocent daydreaming soon got a harsh wakeup call when the reality of being a gay kid, son of a miner, on a tough estate in Sheffield, in a world where the person you want to date better be of the opposite sex because the whole word says so, hit home. It was the seventies and eighties remember. I'm not going to catalogue the pain; you'll think I am exaggerating. You can imagine, however, the bullying, the 'queer bashing', the stereotyping (which one of the Village People are you?) the clandestine life you are forced to follow and, worst of all, the feeling of being a complete disappointment to

108

your father, as a result of simply being true to yourself. Having survived this – remember many didn't – to then get to the world of work, and in education no less; surely there would be more enlightenment, more tolerance and even acceptance? Hell no, here's Section 28. Over to you Maggie[3]: "Children who need to be taught to respect traditional moral values are being taught that they have an inalienable right to be gay. All of those children are being cheated of a sound start in life."

It became illegal to 'promote' homosexuality. It became illegal for me to talk about being me, illegal for me to talk to or help kids going through what I went through. Let's put aside this missed opportunity of being able to really support pupils emotionally, even in just being able to say, 'it'll be ok', and consider the impact on the individual in the workplace.

For me the first few years of being a teacher, middle leader, and even Deputy Head were characterised by fear of stigma, reluctance to talk about my personal life, dread that it would become an issue for my career progression and a general feeling of isolation. Even answers to friendly questions in the staff room of 'what did you get up to at the weekend?' seemed fraught with difficulty. It's hard to imagine nowadays, but in that period, I didn't feel able to be open about myself, because I couldn't be certain of the response I would get. I didn't trust the environment I worked in. Why? Because, apparently, you didn't talk about these things; these were 'outside school' issues and had nothing to do with the workplace and didn't affect you as a teacher or leader. I'd also experienced some pretty awful, though unintentionally so, comments. One that has never left me was said in such a genuinely concerned, (but thoroughly uninformed) 'kind' way by one Headteacher, 'you're gay Steve, you'll die of AIDS, won't you?'. The look of pity in her eyes has never left me.

Some schools and environments were better than others, of course, and I can safely say that I have no proof of actual discrimination because of my sexuality. In an ironic way, because of the nature of intersectionality, of overlapping social identities, in the end it was other factors like age and gender that affected me more, both

---

[3] https://www.independent.co.uk/news/uk/politics/section-28-explained-lgbt-education-schools-homosexuality-gay-queer-margaret-thatcher-a8366741.html

positively and negatively. Positively because as a man in primary there is no doubt that my career progressed because this was seen by some as an 'advantage'. Can you imagine today a Head teacher saying to me as a prospective Deputy 'please apply, I want a man as my Deputy'. (I didn't apply, because if my being a man is more important to you than the fact that I'm bloody good at my job, then no thank you.) I suspect, though again, can't prove, that my gender did play a part in progression and promotions, however.

One thing that certainly did impact me earlier in my career was age. As a successful and ambitious professional, my desire to be a Headteacher was very strong and at 28, having been a deputy for 4 years, I wanted to lead my own school. Knock back after knock back came with the tag, 'governors were really impressed but felt you're just too young'. I wouldn't have cared if they'd said too inexperienced. It was a more enlightened, less risk averse school that finally took the plunge, and the rest, as they say, is history.

Why am I sharing this rather personal narrative right now with you as trust leaders? Not because it's Christmas and I've slipped into Dickens mode, but because the issue of equity, diversity, and inclusion (or lack of it), and other globally relevant issues – such as sustainability – have been thrust into the limelight yet again over the past couple of weeks with all the debate over the upcoming world cup. It's touched a nerve; it's rekindled bad memories and it has made me angry. Angry that people are still subject to much, much worse consequences than I've experienced because of who they are.

Of course, I feel strongly about this subject because of the personal history I've just shared, but I cannot watch the most shameless piece of sports washing in recent times without expressing my anger and sense of sadness, only slightly softened by admiration and gratitude for those who called it out.

Sports washing is a relatively new term, (in 2022, it's Norway's word of the year!) and for those unfamiliar with it, it's used to describe the practice of individuals, groups, corporations, and governments, using sports to improve reputations. Reputations tarnished by failings, wrongdoing, events, actions. It is a way of diverting attention from matters worthy of criticism, such as human rights violations or crimes against humanity.

Although it is a new term, the concept is not new. We are all familiar with whitewashing (needs no explanation), and there's also greenwashing, which is the process of conveying a false impression or misleading information about how a company's products are environmentally sound (in 2021, eleven multinational corporations were called out for doing exactly this.) Its roots, however, probably date back much further to the poet Juvenal at the end of the first Century, with his famous 'give them bread and circuses and the people will never revolt', a reference to distracting from the failings of Roman rule by holding gladiatorial games.

Whatever the etymology, the reality in all these scenarios is that we have a choice in how to respond, both on a personal level and a professional level. We can eat the bread, drink the beer and watch the games and persuade ourselves it's too big an issue for us to do something about, it's someone else's problem, or it's someone else's job at least to tackle it (no pun intended). Or we can embrace the principle that when it comes to human rights, to equality for all, to a belief in the importance of embracing diversity and the absolute necessity for all people to feel they belong, we can accept our own responsibility to play a part, to speak out, to champion, to strive for. And also, to challenge and make a stand when we see abuses which threaten this. Not our business? Not our country? Back to Dickens, A Christmas Carol and Jacob Marley:

"Business? Mankind was my business. The common welfare was my business; charity, mercy, forbearance, and benevolence, were, all my business. The dealings of my trade were but a drop of water in the comprehensive ocean of my business!"

I've watched with admiration, despair, surprise, at how individuals and companies have either made this issue their business or haven't. How each have responded to it. It says a lot about them. It's also prompted me to reflect upon my own response and whether or not I'm satisfied with that.

Whichever answer I settle upon on that particular question, one thing I'm mostly satisfied with is the steps we took at REAch2 on the issues of Equity, Diversity and Inclusion and in recognition that, whilst as CEOs and trust leaders, and thus social leaders, it can be difficult to impact at a macro level, as per the reflection above, we most certainly do have the influence to impact at our own organisational level.

On such a huge subject, I thought it might be useful to share just a few takeaways from my experience of this as CEO and on the importance of the role of the Chair and the Board.

Firstly, even though I knew I felt passionately about EDI, for a long time, I didn't feel confident that I understood all the issues around it, or indeed, had clarity about what it actually meant. I also now know that I didn't make it a priority and take decisive action on it soon enough from fear of getting it wrong.

In all such situations, it's best, I find, to acknowledge a lack of understanding and experience and seek an expert (remember my earlier blog, the CEO needs to be an expert, not THE expert). For us that was Linbert Spencer. He brought the clarity I was lacking.

He helped me understand that the Inclusion, Diversity and Equality Agenda (IDEA) is about managing inclusion, valuing difference, promoting equality of opportunity and combating discrimination. The very act of deconstructing it in this way seemed to make taking action and devising a strategy more doable.

Linbert also helped the whole organisation understand why EDI matters. We were pretty strong on understanding that it's the *morally right* thing and that it's *socially desirable,* but he also helped us realise that in addition to this, it's *economically sensible* and *vitally important for organistions.* There is a whole tranche of research and evidence out there about how commitment and action towards equality and diversity in an inclusive environment is not only good for the business of humankind (sorry Dickens – language has evolved) but for the business of business. Take a look, for example, at the McKinsey research and you'll see startling stats about increased productivity, increased profitability, improved recruitment and retention, increased employee engagement, improved employee wellbeing, more creativity, better teamwork etc. It all adds up to a win on every front.

In all of this work with Linbert in deepening my understanding of these issues, the simplest yet most profound takeaway was an understanding that diversity is simply difference, equality is the right to be different (protected by legislation) but it is a culture of inclusion that enables an individual to *make* a difference. If there is diversity but a culture exists where people are unable or unwilling to speak up or act, then that diversity doesn't mean as much. To fully capitalise on the opportunities diversity presents we must work to create an inclusive culture that allows all members of the school community to contribute their unique perspectives and maximise their potential. This was such a crucial learning point for me and Linbert's assertion that 'inclusion is an emotion, a feeling' took me right back to my early experiences of 'exclusion' and how it negatively affected my ability to be the best version of myself and I knew that he was right, and I knew where I had to start.

Having said this, when I say where 'I' needed to start, if a key takeaway so far is about becoming more expert as CEO and trust leaders in understanding the complex issues surrounding EDI, and finding that expertise outside the organisation if necessary, the next takeaway is the importance, when driving equality, diversity and inclusion, of change starting with the trust Board and in particular the Chair.

One of the obvious starting points is to take stock of how visibly diverse the Board is. I suspect that for many, like it was for us, this can be a bit uncomfortable. It's difficult to defend a commitment to diversity when the Board itself is homogeneous. For better or worse, the composition of the Board sends a strong signal about the organisation's values. Most research shows that to be really effective there has to be a critical mass of diverse viewpoints rather than simply 'symbolic' or ''representative' members and whilst it would be too harsh to say the Board at Reach2 reflected the latter, it very clearly wasn't diverse enough.

It was at the point when – having committed to a real drive on diversity, and on accepting the reality that the Board wasn't diverse enough – three Trustees volunteered to stand down to enable the Chair to recruit, that I knew that the Board was serious about this agenda. It also sent a very strong message to every member of the school community about their commitment to this. Such was the calibre of those standing down, they also volunteered to help in the search to find their replacements with the requisite skills and experience from within their own sector.

One of the strengths of the current Chair of the Board is that he recognises that, as per our takeaway above, just being diverse isn't enough and to maximise the value of this more diverse Board, he must also create the environment that encourages participation from all members. He does this really well by being genuinely curious about different points of view and experiences and open minded about decisions to be taken.

Another way in which a Board helps drive the EDI agenda is by making their business the CEOs business. Setting the tone that EDI is important to the organisation by keeping it on the board agenda, asking probing questions about efforts to improve equality, diversity and inclusion (I remember one particularly challenging question about the career flight paths of diverse talent and how this is managed), and by being all over the data. Through activity such as this, Chairs and Boards really can, I believe, have a direct impact on success.

And so, briefly onto the role of the CEO in all this. I'm not going to focus on the organisational aspects of driving this agenda, be that; putting structures and practices into place to encourage inclusive working environments and provide diverse talent with the support and systems they need to be successful, policies that enshrine equality and protect against discrimination, management activities such as gathering data and setting targets etc. to inform our action, or even building that inclusive culture I talked about last month. All of this is documented elsewhere.

I'm going to share, instead, what has been my own personal, very intentional strategy for the last twenty-five years both as a headteacher, and CEO. It's a very simple strategy, and many won't be comfortable with it, but I believe in it passionately.

Me being me gives a mandate for you being you

This is why pretty much any person who has come into contact with me, worked with me, encountered me at a conference, followed me on Twitter, all that stuff, will know things I think it's important they know: I'm gay, I have white working-class roots, I'm 59, I'm spiritual not religious, I was civil partnered and so on. All the characteristics of intersectionality. All the things that make me diverse.

This is not because I like over sharing, don't understand boundaries or can't control myself. It's because I know how I personally want to contribute to the EDI agenda. You will, I hope, have your own ways.

I've covered a fair bit in the last few pages, so where did all this reflection and musing begin? Ah yes, once upon a time...
Well, just in case you were worried, the fairy tale I started with had a happy ending after all.

After many years of a strained relationship, one phone call out of the blue changed everything. The father called his son and said, 'I don't understand your lifestyle, but I am trying, and you are my son and I love you; that's all that matters, can we talk?' Thus, the healing began, and they became absolute best friends for the last twenty years of the father's life, so in true tradition of Christmas and fairy tales, happily ever after.

I'm proud of my father who overcame so many prejudices, as we all need to, who learned to rethink stereotypes, as we all need to, who ultimately made sure there was a safe place for me to be me, and the very best version of me, as we all need to for each other.

The great thing is, as CEOs the power is in our hands to be able to do this for so many people, and we must make it our business to drive the changes needed.

WINNING MOVES

∞ Ensure the Board signals the importance of equality, diversity and inclusion by making its commitment explicit and accepting collective accountability for outcomes. Keep membership of the board under review to ensure that there are diverse viewpoints rather than just symbolic or representative members. Make EDI part of core business by setting organisational goals and defining key metrics of success as with other critical strategies. Ensure EDI is on all Board agendas.

∞ Embrace the opportunity to contribute positively to the EDI agenda on both a personal and organisational level. Recognise the symbolic importance of the CEO making a stand and taking action. Lead by example and make this a personal initiative. Publicly live your own diversity and encourage this in others.

∞ Recognise that this is such a complex societal issue that the expertise you need will probably sit both within and outside the organisation. Seek an expert who can offer advice and be an objective critical friend. Aim to make a meaningful contribution to your organisation's development but recognise that it is a long-term strategy and will go on past your tenure.

Appendix A

Sir Steve Lancashire' Speech to the National #TrustLeaders CEO Conference 2022. The speech was delivered in Nottingham on 22nd September 2022.

Good morning.

What an absolute privilege it is to be here today amongst so many of our CEO network members and Forum Strategy colleagues to share with you what I hope will be a very special day. It's a day where we can reconnect with each other after the summer break, take joy in the comradery that always exists when we meet, take comfort from knowing that we are amongst supportive colleagues who share the same challenges we do as Trust leaders, and take courage from the fact that as a network we are here to face these challenges together and find our way forward, together.

Many of you will know this is the first year in ten years that I have not started September as a Chief Executive, having stepped down this summer from what has been undoubtedly the most challenging but rewarding role of my career, to pursue two great passions of mine – on a personal front – travel, because it's true that it really does broaden the mind and nourish the soul (something I feel I need after a relentless few years) and professionally, to use the knowledge, skills and experience I've gained as a Chief Exec to try and help and support those currently in the role, thinking of moving into this role or in another senior position in a Trust.

In a sector about learning I'm keen that my learning is used to help others. And it's a sector I have always been passionate about. What a privilege it is to have the opportunity to be a positive influence on so many young lives, so many families and communities across the country. What a privilege, also, to be the guardian of those who work for us, our leaders, our teachers, our support staff: to nurture them, safeguard their well-being, guide their careers, help them when they are struggling and celebrate with them when they succeed.

But of course, with this privilege comes great responsibility. A responsibility to be the very best leader that we can for the people in our care, a responsibility to ensure that we create the greatest schools that we can for our children to learn in, our staff to work in and our communities to turn to and have confidence in, and a responsibility to clear away all the problems that stand in the way of us doing these two things.

And herein lies the rub of course, because this is a tough job, and the problems and challenges are acute. From the round table we held a couple of weeks ago and the results of the Cost-of-Living Survey carried out by our partners at The Key, together with Forum Strategy, it is clear we are all feeling the pressures of what is a very challenging context right now.

Let's briefly reflect on what these challenges are...

Undoubtedly, pretty much everyone in this room and beyond is feeling the impact of the cost-of-living crisis, whether this is rising energy prices, food prices, inflation, rent increases, you name it. And to be honest, if people in this room, including me, are feeling the impact of it, let's remember how it must be for those in our most disadvantaged areas, those on low wages, those who are vulnerable – the very families that many of us serve.

Add to this what is a very real health and wellbeing crisis amongst many people and particularly young people. I was so sad last week, which was suicide awareness week, to read how many young people took their own lives last year, many seeing no other way out. And to read how help lines are being swamped by calls from families desperate for support. For example, I was stunned to be told that at Reach2 last year calls to our Employee Assistance Programme had increased ten-fold in one year and this is from families who, you could imagine, are probably better placed than most to weather this.

On a macro level, there is the political uncertainty and turmoil we are experiencing, which not only impacts on our personal lives, but our professional lives too. How many Secretaries of States in how many weeks? Almost farcical. My favourite being a Secretary of State appointed at the start of the summer holidays and replaced in September. Tough gig.

And on the theme of politics, my view is the same as the rest of the Forum Strategy team, the Government's White Paper and the DfE's policies do not yet fully cover the challenges we face now or the key trends of the coming years including the issues I've just noted but also challenges such as likely economic and labour market changes, climate change and sustainability issues. There's also the ticking time bomb, discussed at the round table, of the need for a once in a generation investment, of significant proportions, to make the education estates sustainable and fit for purpose. I was having discussions with Lord Nash on this very issue eight years ago, and we are no nearer a proper solution.

Finally, before I depress us all, there is a real need to herald in a new era of respect for the profession from government. A need to create a strong dialogue over the issues I've covered so that we don't get the kind of surprises we got this summer over pay rises etc. The job is tough enough without this kind of last-minute curveball.

I'm teasing, of course, about depressing you all, as I list the multiple challenges that face us, but it is imperative that we are realistic about the scale of the challenge ahead so that our response can be robust and commensurate with the task at hand.

But colleagues, I am speaking honestly when I say, I am not depressed or disheartened about the journey that lies ahead. (Those friends who like to tease me are not allowed to shout out 'That's because you're not doing the job any more Steve').

Let me say again. I really am not depressed or disheartened about it. In fact I feel quite the opposite, I feel invigorated and excited. Why do I feel like this? because I have hope.

I want to use the rest of this speech to talk about why hope is so important and why the hope and optimism I have is well founded I

119

believe. There are many definitions of the concept/virtue/ characteristic of hope, and I suspect it means something slightly different to all of us.

I think I first really came upon the concept through my love of reading and fascination for Greek Mythology. I wanted to be Mighty Zeus and defeat all the Titans (No delusions of grandeur then!) and a particular favourite story was of Prometheus stealing (my!) fire.

For those of you who have forgotten the legend, Prometheus and his brother Epimetheus were Titans but pledged their loyalty to Zeus and the Olympians. Zeus rewarded them for their loyalty and gave them the job of creating the first creatures to live on Earth. Epimetheus formed the animals and gave each a special skill and form of protection. Prometheus took his time moulding man and was left with no forms of protection since Epimetheus had already given them all away. He knew man needed some form of protection and asked Zeus if he could let man have fire. Zeus refused. Fire was only for the gods. Prometheus ignored Zeus and gave man fire anyway.

For this, Prometheus was punished. Zeus tied him with chains to a rock far away in the Caucasus Mountains where nobody would find him. Every day Zeus sent an eagle to feast upon Prometheus' liver, which grew back every day so that Prometheus would have to endure this torture daily until Heracles found Prometheus and killed the eagle and let Prometheus go. This torture wasn't enough of a punishment for Zeus who also believed that humans should be punished for accepting the gift of fire from Prometheus. To punish man, Zeus created a woman named Pandora. She was moulded to look like the beautiful goddess Aphrodite. She received the gifts of wisdom, beauty, kindness, peace, generosity, and health from the gods.

Zeus brought her to Earth to be Epimetheus' wife. Even though Epimetheus' brother, Prometheus, had warned him of Zeus' trickery and told him not to accept gifts from the gods, Epimetheus was too taken with her beauty and wanted to marry her anyway. As a wedding present, Zeus gave Pandora a box but warned her never to open it. Pandora, who was created to be curious, couldn't stay away from the box and the urge to open it became too strong. Horrible things flew out of the box including greed, envy, hatred, pain, disease, hunger, poverty, war, and death. All of life's miseries had been let out into the world.

Pandora slammed the lid of the box back down. The last thing remaining inside of the box was hope.

Ever since, according to the legend, humans have been able to hold onto this hope in order to survive the wickedness that Pandora had let out. Now I'm not suggesting of course that the acute challenges I talked about earlier are on the same scale as some of the nasties that came out of the box, but I love the way this story exemplifies that it is Hope that is the antidote and, if you like, defence or weapon against feeling overwhelmed by all the difficult, bad stuff.

In a rather more clinical, less literary way, dictionaries call it something like 'a feeling of expectation and desire for a particular thing to happen' or a variation of this. So, more emphasis on it looking toward the future, and usually, a more desirable future. Many people have used this idea. Barack Obama:

'Hope is that thing inside us that insists, despite all evidence to the contrary, that something better awaits us if we have the courage to reach for it, and to work for it, and to fight for it.'

It is this latter description I think that gets more to the heart of where we need to be because it acknowledges that hope needs to be accompanied by action, by deeds, by hard work, and even by (metaphorically) fighting, and we don't passively wait for this better future to happen.

And it is this final definition of hope I'm going to share which leads me to the belief that as Trust Leaders, you will lead us to this better future:

'Hope is to want something to happen and have a good reason to think that it will.'

I have a good reason to think all of you in this room can deliver this better future, why?

Because: 'You've just done it, you're still doing it, and you'll carry on doing it'

The way in which as a sector, as a network, as individual leaders you have all come together and have tackled some of the most complex, most challenging, most heart-breaking problems facing our schools and their communities over the last few years leaves me in no doubt that my hope is well founded.

Let's explore a bit more...

The pandemic and our ongoing challenges have facilitated some fairly seismic shifts. I want to explore three and in doing so note some remarkable achievements that are at the heart of why I say our hope is well founded.

Firstly, we have started to break down the artificial barriers, the legal constructs, the insular mindsets that have been a feature of our educational landscape for too long. We have begun to collaborate, network, co-operate more than ever and now understand that we are all stronger and better as a result of sharing our knowledge, our expertise, our resources and, even, at times, ourselves as leaders. We have 'open sourced' ourselves to each other, put aside personal (and Trust) agendas and egos and committed ourselves to the common good. The results have been, and will continue to be, phenomenal. We have collectively survived (not without hurt and loss, of course) a pandemic, we are now working hard to find solutions to the challenges of austerity, political turmoil, financial hardship, all the things I listed earlier.

And despite all of this, we are here together today talking about the future, about what more we can do to serve our school communities. Past challenges are exactly that and we are ready to take what we have collectively learned and apply it to solving our next set of challenges. This is hopeful leadership.

The next seismic shift has been in our ability to innovate, to change our ways of working, to be creative and solve problems we didn't even know existed. We can now believe much more in the art of the possible. The challenges we have faced and overcome have pushed us in a direction we perhaps knew we should be going, just much quicker, and it has shown us our true potential.

Let's just take a moment to reflect on just two of these accomplishments.

Pretty much a digital transformation has taken place where, challenged by necessity, we rethought traditional models of teaching and learning, moved to a hybrid model of blended online and classroom learning with astonishing speed. We upskilled ourselves to meet this new way of working, we rewrote curriculums to make sure we were meeting the changing needs of our children and young people, and we solved the logistical problems of multi-site schooling. Of course, this was supported by central government putting their hands in the public pocket to give us some of the tech we needed but the essential problem of how to school pupils in extraordinary circumstances was solved by the sector working together and finding collective solutions.

And now that a degree of normality has returned to our schools, look how well we have all put provision in place to support those pupils who have had their learning disrupted or who perhaps fared less well. Look how well we have put support in place to support the most vulnerable, to help them continue to thrive and learn. This is a sector who are experts in what they do.

Let's look at the way in which our working practices changed and our realisation that we could do things differently if we challenged traditional norms. And the realisation that this could really have an impact on some of those complex issues we are struggling with such as environmental sustainability and organisational efficiency. Through our teams and staff working differently across the organisation, in my last year as Chief Executive at Reach2, we knocked a million pounds off our travel budget alone. Money that can be spent on addressing other challenges and what a reduction in our environmental footprint. It is because of this proven ability to innovate, to adapt, to be creative in finding solutions that I once again can say how confident I am in a hopeful future.

I think the final seismic shift which I'll touch on briefly because I could write a book on it and have covered it in a couple of blogs is probably less a seismic shift and more a forceful reminder that schools are the centre of their school communities, and we are civic leaders. In the communities that we serve we are a mainstay for our families, they turn to us in times of need, they look to us to help solve their problems.

In my blog about the masterclass of leadership Her Majesty the Queen gave us, I talk about her being a constant in peoples' lives, well we are that constant for our school communities and in these most challenging of times we need to be at our very best and it is imperative, as I said in last week's blog, that what matters most to our families, matters most to us.

At the start of this speech, I talked about being invigorated and excited about the future. I hope, through what I have been describing, and our collective belief in the power of connection and community that you are too.

Christopher Reeve, AKA Superman, who many know went through a horrific accident that changed his life, once said *'hope is a choice and once you choose hope anything is feasible'*.

He also developed what he called 'habits of hope' a concept later developed by others.

It's an idea that really resonated with me and includes behaviours I consciously tried to adopt both as a CEO and as a person. Let me conclude by sharing three of them and at the same time ask you to reflect on how important they might be in your roles as the most senior people in your organisations, as the standard bearers of hope.

Focusing on the opportunities, not just the restrictions of any situation

I was heartened when I saw that a third of respondents to the Cost-of-Living Survey had highlighted the positive outcomes, even be they unintended consequences, of the challenging times we have been through, with innovation, increased efficiency and sustainability all being positively impacted. The innovations I listed earlier. Again, last week at the round table, the excellent examples of Trust leaders being creative in how to do more with less. If we have more thinking like this, more seizing of these opportunities then that 'belief, wish combined with action' will mean that hopeful leadership will have a much better chance of delivering that better future.

Cultivating optimism

The old glass half full or half empty scenario. I love that analogy of either being a mood hoover or a radiator. Trying to light up the room with warmth and positivity rather than being like a Harry Potter dementor sucking all hope and joy out of the world. There's quite a lot of research out there that shows that if you're optimistic you have a better quality of life and even a better psychological state. If you're a leader asking people to go the extra mile through tough times, my belief is that by focusing on the positive, celebrating the gains is the best way to give them hope and motivate them to action.

Doing random acts of kindness

I think kindness gives hope to others especially if it's unexpected because it reinforces that people are essentially good and this is such a positive thing. I feel great when someone does something kind for me and I hope they feel the same. Throughout the pandemic one of my mantras was 'be kind' and I tried to act on this as much as I could. Given how influential we are in our role as Trust leaders, the smallest things can make a big difference.

So, in summary...

It's often been quoted to me that 'hope is not a strategy'. Well, I don't hold with that, and to my mind, 'hopeful leadership' based on the understanding we have of it being a wish, a desire, an expectation of a better future delivered through our actions, is exactly where we should be right now, and exactly what is going to see us through these next few years, and I ask that you all be 'hopeful leaders'.

I'll leave you with Charles Dickens:
'It's always something to know you've done the most you could, but don't leave off hoping or it's no use doing anything. Hope, hope to the last!'

Thank you.

Appendix B

A tribute to Her Majesty Queen Elizabeth II and reflections on the cost-of-living crisis (a blog from September 2023)

Little did we know, that when those of us attending the Forum Strategy #TrustLeaders roundtable event on Wednesday were discussing the pressures on schools and Trusts and the challenges of operating in an uncertain, volatile world, that that world was about to become even more unsettled with the death of Her Majesty, the Queen. In the short term at least. We don't know what, if any, direct impact it will have on our professional or personal lives longer term but it has given us some immediate challenges; such as an extra school closure day, and a decision about how to approach it with our pupils, colleagues and staff to comfort (because if your experience is the same as mine, the strength of feeling and depth of sorrow this has caused has caught us all a little by surprise).

For us as CEOs and leaders, these are all quite manageable of course, and when this very sad event has passed, the same professional challenges we discussed at the roundtable event are still with us. I'll come onto some thoughts on this a little later. First, with your indulgence, I'd like to pay my own respects to Her Majesty by sharing my thoughts on part of her legacy that I hope isn't overlooked and that is: she gave us a masterclass in brilliant leadership. Here's a few thoughts as to why. *(I do want to acknowledge that views on the monarchy can divide people, and I offer the below as an observation of leadership, and nothing else.)*

Firstly, I believe she was the embodiment of servant leadership. I think she understood that she was there for the people, not the other way round. Her biographer described her as having an 'almost a crippling sense of duty' and I think this manifested itself in many ways. Firstly, in the sheer number of commitments she undertook throughout her life, and right up to the last few days of her life. Secondly in the number of patronages to charities and public sector organisations she gave, the commensurate way she undertook royal duties and even, symbolic as it may be, joining the auxiliary territorial services as a driver and mechanic.

All this adds up to someone who understands that others come first, and the really important question is 'what can I do for you?'. In terms of personal characteristics, I think this servant leadership quality was shown in her curiosity for people and things, her empathy, her ability to listen and ask questions and her commitment to the national community. My favourite respectful cartoon of The Queen this week was a picture of her with a tartan skirt, handbag, corgis at side, standing at the feet of an enormous elderly figure shrouded in white at the pearly gates and her asking, 'and what do you do?'

Secondly, she showed great strength in the face of adversity; she was that immutable rock on which the waves crashed and broke. Whatever our views on the monarchy and her as Queen, as a leader she faced some pretty formidable and turbulent international and national events; from the war to JFKs assassination, the moon landing, 9/11, Brexit, the Covid pandemic and of course, family tragedies. Throughout it all, she seems to me to have had an immutable strength of character, a calmness and stoicism, a determination to 'get through' things. In her own words, *'when life seems hard, the courageous do not lie down and accept defeat, they are all the more determined to struggle for a better future.'* Many people are recognising that she has been a constant in our lives and what a good thing this has been. How often have we talked about the need for the leaders to be that strong, immovable, confidence giving figure? I can't think of a better role model for these characteristics.

One of those 'make or break' characteristics in great leaders for me is personal authenticity, particularly when it comes to values and how an individual's actions match up with these. I talked in my last blog about how credibility is easily lost when there's a mismatch – think party gate. One of the most powerful images of the last couple of years is The Queen sat alone, in mourning, at her husband's funeral. Following the law, not abusing her power or position but doing the right thing. Of course, people will say she had to; everyone was watching her. But my favourite definition of integrity being 'doing the right thing even when no one is looking', my belief is cameras aside, she would have done the same thing because I believe she had a strong moral code. Why do I think this? Because *over time* and *in different contexts* her actions were consistent and she did what she said she believed in: her duties as monarch, hard work, leading by example.

Next, The Queen embraced change, recognising that it is inevitable and that strong leaders do embrace it, seeing it not as an obstacle but an opportunity for growth and development. In her own words, 'I have lived long enough to know that things never remain quite the same for very long'. The world has changed beyond recognition since her coronation and there are some great examples of how she has kept up with these shifts, from her first battle with Winston Churchill over breaking with tradition and televising her coronation rather than having it covered on radio, ('I need to be seen to be believed') to reportedly being the first Head of State to send an email in 1976, and more recently the modernisation of the monarchy.

Finally, I hope this will make you smile, I suspect The Queen has been pretty good at succession planning. Of course, she hasn't had the tricky task of interviewing and selecting her successor and there isn't a Board of Trustees to answer to for this. More, the British public, in time. But from watching both King Charles and Prince William and their talk of modernising the monarchy, and of the need to be ever more in touch and responsive with the British public, I suspect she has been doing what every great leader does; preparing for the future when they are no longer there.

My own personal experience of meeting the Queen was a very special day for my family and I, and I was left in awe of her absolute professionalism, her warmth, her ability to make one feel individually important, even amongst a multitude of people, and that most important leadership trait, (self-deprecating) humour. In my conversation with her about my CEO role she had clearly been well briefed and commented 'I understand you run 52 schools, (correct at the time), you can't possibly do all that yourself. I suppose you're rather like me and have other people to do most of the hard work!' Indeed Ma'am. R.I.P.

The theme of this blog was originally to be about strategic planning, setting long-term goals etc. That was before a whole load of issues landed at your doorsteps manifesting into some really pressing issues in the here and now. I was really pleased, therefore, that we were able to hold the round table event last week to be responsive to the challenges you're facing. In very brief summary for those who haven't seen the paper or couldn't attend, the issues centred on the rising costs of energy, the need for a fair price cap, and the difficulties associated with grants. The pay rises for teaching and support staff, the ridiculously late notice of this and how they are to be funded, the generally dire condition of school estates and the challenge of making them efficient and sustainable, and the real feeling that there isn't – at present – a meaningful dialogue with central government on these issues. On a more macro level our school communities are faced with a cost-of-living crisis and the associated impact this has on well-being and health. At Forum Strategy, as a first step, we have turned this into a paper and made representation with it to central government.

In listening to the comments and observations of our networks, it's clear that as trust leaders you are being creative and rigorous in trying to solve these issues. As I reflect on the conversations, some general observations occur about what I think is important right now.

My first observation picks upon a theme I highlighted earlier; the importance of the ultimate leader (CEO) in being the rock of the organisation, bringing confidence, finding the path forward and keeping things in perspective. What really struck me from peoples' comments was the pragmatic way these challenges are being faced and the lack of panic. Spot on. There's a moment in one of the Harry Potter books where Harry produces a really powerful spell and he is able to produce it because, through a trick of time, he has done it before, and this gives him confidence to do it again and even better. Same here, we have faced equally difficult challenges, found solutions and we will again. Some of them will be of our own making, some government led (stepping in with a six-month solution is inadequate but there will be more, I'm convinced of it) and some problems will just resolve themselves; they do that sometimes.

Our job as CEOs is to weather this, do the best we can and focus on making sure our people are OK. They will be looking to us and need that confidence and reassurance we can bring. One of the advantages of being a long in the tooth CEO is understanding that history repeats itself, that governments need schools open and that when there's a lot of noise in the system, solutions are found. I think we are at that point which is why representing these sector issues as we have just done is really important.

I have also got to be real about this, however. There isn't going to be a magic money tree that solves all our fiscal problems and there are some things incumbent on us. One of those is in securing optimal organisational efficiency and best use of resources at the same time as making best use of partnerships and both formal and informal working arrangements with other organisations. It was heartening to hear just how many leaders in our network are already doing this but one challenge I would like to pose is how often we really evaluate how efficient our current structures, processes, resource allocation, ways of doing things etc. are and how often we default to historic assumptions or working practices. In such a fiscally challenged context, and in such a volatile environment, there's an argument that we now need to think more about zero based budgeting where all expenditure is evaluated and needs to be justified so that, as well as optimising revenue, we optimise costs. In some cases, this is going to mean tough decisions and new ways of doing things, but I think we are in a position of needs must.

On a similar note, there's a thistle to be grasped for some CEOs and that is in ensuring that the fiscal benefits of being in a MAT are fully realised. I find that in many MATS there is a strong culture of collaboration around teaching and learning, professional development, curriculum etc. However, still, many have not moved to pooled funding, centralised procurement, rationalised and shared staffing structures. The argument against this is often centred on loss of autonomy, loss of identity for individual schools and other cultural issues. The reality is, in this climate, in terms of securing maximum economies of scale and least financial and resource (human and other) duplication, and therefore best value for money, these 'internal' resourcing arrangements do need to be considered to ensure that the MAT secures best value and is optimally efficient. It's the area I support with most when mentoring CEOs, because it's a thorny one.

Given that this blog was to be about strategic planning, I'd like to make a brief observation on it, because it's pertinent to the issue of dealing with volatile and challenging contexts. In looking back at my attempts at planning over the last ten years as CEO, I find I have written three five-year plans, a 2-year plan and a number of annual plans. Yep, the maths doesn't work, so either I can't add up or my long-term plans never fully came to fruition. It's the latter of course. To me this signals that the days of a guaranteed steady state are gone and that we need to look at strategic planning in a different way. Historically, in drafting our strategies we have all pretty much followed a similar process and model. Think about a future state, define a multi-year plan to achieve that future state, call upon the organisation to execute a plan, monitor performance to keep everyone on track, and evaluate success. I wonder how many of us this has worked for over the last few years?

In these turbulent times I think it is time to reconsider what good strategy looks like and to start to think of strategy making as a continuous process that generates a living, dynamic plan that is able to be responsive to changing conditions and events. Many business organisations have moved to this model, and I think it has interesting implications for us. In this there is a recognition that long term aspirations need to be set (and left alone) but that the real focus should be on actions that close the gap between the reality now and longer-term ambitions and this should be evaluated again when the new reality exists and when each set of actions has been taken. In this process, monitoring doesn't ask the question 'how are we performing?', rather, 'do we need to alter course?' in order to achieve longer term ambitions. It's a subtle difference and recognises that there is a constant state of flux, and more flexible strategies will be required with more agile and less fixed strategy making.

My final observation is around the resonance between what organisations prioritise in times of turbulence and what the communities they serve are experiencing and need, for if we are truly to serve then they should be in accord. The one big mistake I always thought the Queen made was in being too late in responding in a way the country needed to the death of the Princess of Wales. It's notable that when she did alter her course and respond differently, she later talked of mistakes in leadership and lessons to be learned (something a great leader is able to do). As a result of listening and responding, however, her position as a great leader was further consolidated, I believe. Now, of course, I'm not suggesting that we are in a similar position right now, but many communities are under strain and peoples' lives are becoming increasingly difficult. We are perfectly placed to respond positively to this and be a force for good by doing our very best for the people we have a responsibility to and in the way they need. We can only do this if we prioritise the right things and as we start this new school year and start to roll out our plans my advice would be to listen to those we serve and respond.

Appendix C

Imposter Syndrome and New Year's Resolutions
(a blog from January 2023)

One of the many joys of being Chair of the national #TrustLeaders CEO network, delivering on the Being the CEO programme and all of the individual mentoring sessions I'm currently undertaking is having the opportunity to work professionally with a really diverse, talented, extraordinarily committed, and just downright impressive set of people. Oh, by the way, in case you don't recognise yourself, that's you reading this. Yes, YOU!

For those who know me well, you know I can be a charmer, can work a room or an audience and, as my mum would say, 'Have the gift of the gab'. 'You should sell cars' she used to say 'Because you could sell coal to miners´ (and other idioms). I actually prefer the Oxford Dictionary definition of this phrase 'Gift of the gab' which is 'the ability to speak with eloquence and fluency.' But I'm quite sure my mother didn't mean this.

Whatever she did mean, those (dubious) attributes I mention above are not needed here. Because I'm very genuine when I say that the sector is in good hands when I see just how well our trusts are being led, how there's an ever-increasing willingness to collaborate for the greater good and how some very substantial problems are being overcome, all with such spirit and humour.

One of the interesting things about working with so many CEOs is that you start to see trends and commonalities, so the reason that I feel the need to emphasise that it is YOU I am talking about is that one of these consistent themes I've picked up is CEOs experiencing 'impostor syndrome' (AKA impostor phenomenon or impostorism). We are all probably aware that this is a psychological occurrence in which an individual doubts their skills, talents, or accomplishments and has a persistent internalised fear of being exposed as a fraud, believing their success to be as a result of luck or other factors rather than their own competencies. What I wasn't aware of is that when impostor syndrome was first conceptualised, it was viewed as a phenomenon that was common among high-achieving women.

The term was first introduced in an article published in 1978, (The Impostor Phenomenon in High Achieving Women) and was based on research on women in higher education and professional industries. All of the participants had been formally recognised for their professional excellence by colleagues and displayed academic achievement through educational degrees and standardised testing scores. Despite the consistent external validation these women received, they lacked internal acknowledgement of their accomplishments. When asked about their success, some participants, as noted above, attributed it to luck, while some believed that people had overestimated their capabilities. There's been a lot more research into the phenomenon since the 1970s and the general consensus is that it's something which is not particularly gender based with more recent research finding that impostorism is spread equally among men and women. Based on my somewhat more limited experience I would tend to agree with this; I come across it fairly equally amongst the men and women CEOs I work with.

What has remained consistent, however, is what researchers call the 'distinguishing characteristics' which are indicators that suggest someone might be feeling this. These indicators include fear of failure, denial of ability, feeling fear and guilt about success on one hand and on the over compensatory side, the need to be the best, to exert superhuman characteristics in order to be the best. For anyone who does fit this description, you're in good company with many high-profile people (Barack Obama, Tom Hanks, Jacinda Ardern to name a few) all publicly speaking about it.

And from Maya Angelou "I have written 11 books, but each time I think, 'Uh oh, they're going to find out now. I've run a game on everybody, and they're going to find me out.'
So, what's the point of me telling you all this? Well research also shows that circa 70 percent of people experience this in a professional context and that it can be a barrier to them achieving their full potential. (Research does also suggest that some go on to be a super achiever as a result of it but in much fewer numbers). And once again,

the first figure feels about right to me. Believe me when I say I come across this a lot. I'm not suggesting that in these cases it is getting in the way of people being the very best version of themselves, but it most certainly is a factor on several fronts, be that lack of confidence, overreliance on others' judgement, fear of taking risks etc.

The other reason I'm telling you this is that a couple of the ways of overcoming this (apparently, there are about a dozen) are firstly to take explicit note, regularly, both in the short and long term, of your accomplishments. To *notice* when you are successful on whatever scale and start to internalise this success. I often, in mentoring sessions, ask CEOs to reflect on this and talk me through their achievements. I did the same with those who worked for me when I was still CEO.

Another way brings me back to where I started – accept the compliment when it comes from someone who is an 'expert' in the field (of course I'm not claiming to be this, my mum would have given me a severe stare and say stop showing off! But I do know a great CEO when I see one and I'm seeing a lot of great CEOs as I said earlier). So, please, accept the compliment without qualification, without deflection, without embarrassment.

I've chosen this topic both because I'm coming across it frequently and also because, to extend the theme, it's the time of year (it's New Year as I write this particular blog) when we make resolutions about betterment both on a personal level, and – usually because our work is such an integral part of who we are – a professional and even organisational level too.

The New Year is a significant temporal milestone in the calendar when, as we all know, many people (including me) set new goals for the year ahead. (A bit of digging shows some interesting stats – by country one of the lowest is the US with approx. 35% of adults reporting that they do, one of the highest is Australia with over 70% reporting the same, with the UK somewhere in the middle with just over 50%. There's lots of other variations too according to gender, socioeconomic group, ethnicity etc.)

Whether you make them or not, New Year pledges or promises are not new. Historically, the first recorded people to set pledges (later to become known as resolutions) were apparently the Ancient Babylonians some 4000 years ago. They were also the first civilisation to hold recorded celebrations in honour of the new year, though this began in March not January to coincide with the planting of the crops. The Babylonians are said to have initiated the tradition of a 12-day new year festival called Akitu. Statues of the deities were paraded through the streets and rites were enacted to symbolise victory over chaos (Fitting!). During this festival people pledged their allegiance to the king and made promises to repay debts in the year ahead. They believed if they fulfilled their new year promises then the Gods would look favourably upon them in the year ahead. Ancient Rome continued the tradition of celebrating the new year and setting pledges initially set on the 15th of March (Beware the Ides of March!) but it was Julius Caesar who introduced the Julian Calendar in 46 BC, and declared 1st January as the start of the New Year to honour the Roman God Janus and his two faces, one looking back on the previous year and one looking to the new year. Janus was the protector of doors, archways, thresholds, and transitions into new beginnings.

And chivalry is not dead, in the Middle Ages mediaeval knights pledged their allegiance and renewed their vows to chivalry and knightly valour each new year. Legend has it the most celebrated chivalry vows were called the 'Vow of the Peacock'. The knights placed their hands on a live or roast peacock and renewed their vows to maintain knighthood values throughout the next year. Makes me rather glad I joined this order much, much later. (As an aside, and as a nod to a couple of CEOs who tease me on this subject, I garnered that last bit of information from the Imperial Society of the Knights Bachelor into which you are welcomed on your investiture.)

Even after 4000 years, the new year then continues to symbolise a new threshold, an opportunity for betterment and improvement and even though contemporary resolutions tend to be more secular there's no reason why this still shouldn't be a chance for us, like Janus, to look back at our achievements to date (and note and internalise them, to take credit without flinching remember) and to look at how in the next year, we might better ourselves as CEOs and in doing so our organisations.

I am going to beg your indulgence and forbearance here because I'm going to take an enormous liberty. I'm going to propose three resolutions for us all. Offered in a spirit of affection and playful provocation. I've been looking at the resolutions of the CEOs of some big companies out of sector and thought about their significance for the context we find ourselves in right now, I've reflected on the conversations I've had recently with members of our network as they reflect on what lies ahead and I've reflected on what I need right now. So here goes...

Our **first resolution** is to be fundamentally happy with ourselves as CEOs. Recognise that there is no 'ideal' or 'perfect' CEO and that learning to be the CEO takes time, investment in ourselves and our own learning and that along the way we will make mistakes. 'Progress, not perfection' is what we will seek. As part of this we will recognise that being happy with the way *we* are is good for positive and effective leadership because it leads to a positive mindset and positive actions which helps create a positive culture, infectious across the organisation.

As part of this self-compassion, we are going to nurture our personal resilience, our ability to bounce back from change and challenge. To do this we will focus on our inner landscape as opposed to our outer circumstances focusing more on our reaction to events than to the events themselves, understanding that events, both good and bad, are a constant feature of our professional lives. We will learn to become more aware of what trigger points cause us stress and what serves to nourish us and bring positive emotions.

We will learn to focus more on our achievements than our failures and, because physical and mental resilience need us to keep good habits, we will build these in a meaningful way into our lives, be that through exercise, reading, eating well, socialising, or switching off. (See the clever way I've built the usual list of NY resolutions into this; you don't get off as easy as 'I'll go to the gym more'). And we will reconnect with our inner child. In a world that lacks certainty, as adults we can feel insecure and paralysed by indecision; children are much more comfortable going with the flow and seeing where the journey takes them. We will embrace this uncertainty and start the new year with child-like enthusiasm.

Our **second resolution** has its genesis in the many conversations I've recently had with CEOs on the rather brilliant thread on Twitter from

Geoff&MargaretToo (@RetirementTale5) who share their thoughts after 'A lifetime in education and a year of answering The Call'. A synopsis of their views would be that the entire education system from early years to higher education appears to be in a very fragile state, even broken in places, life has changed profoundly in schools and the new normal is disruption, uncertainty and constant challenge. The workforce is changing, and a great many people are struggling. The Government acts as though the pandemic is over, and that life has returned to normal and the DfE has resumed its pre-pandemic expectations of schools, teachers and leaders.

The political leadership of education in recent years has been to everybody's detriment and has resulted in a complete lack of vision and understanding and school leaders are left in a bewildering mess. Strong stuff indeed, you may or may not agree. From my conversations with colleagues certainly some of it resonates and in particular one issue that has come through strongly to me is the agitation that the White paper and Schools Bill (and the subsequent abandonment) has caused for trust leaders, particularly around the issue of growth of trusts and the rationalisation of the sector by the DfE. One close CEO colleague asked me 'What do you do in a situation like this?' My answer lies in our second resolution:

No longer will we be like Autolycus, a feather for each wind that blows, rather we will use this uncertainty to bring clarity about who we are, why we exist and how we want to operate. We will reflect on our mission, vision and values to ensure we are staying true to ourselves and our purpose. To ensure we are ethical, act with integrity and set the best possible example as societal leaders.

We will think about what is important to us and what isn't, and we will listen to those we serve, our children, families, and communities to ensure we are doing our very best for them, and they, and nothing else, are our priority. We will ignore, dismiss or find a way around anything that hinders this. In practical terms, we will make sure that our strategies and plans are completely aligned with this. And we will be the best possible advocate for them, for ourselves and for the sector, even if this means we have to raise our head above the parapet and speak out both individually and collectively.

As CEOs we will remember that now is the time for humane leadership, that emotional and economic recovery is needed both in the world at large and in our own organisations. Our people are crying out for courageous and compassionate leadership, and we will be the very embodiment of this, remembering that if we prioritise employee welfare, fair treatment and genuine care we build a healthy culture that benefits us all.

When we do all these things, then, as from Ephesians 4, we will no longer be 'infants, tossed back and forth by the waves, and blown here and there by every wind of teaching and by the cunning and craftiness of people in their deceitful scheming.' (I'll leave you to fill in the blanks as to who these crafty people might be). We will instead fix our true North and steer our ship accordingly.

In setting new year resolutions, the focus is often on ourselves and our families and is usually about personal betterment which is always laudable. Our third and final resolution, however, is much more about the greater good. It's not new, but it is needed now more than ever, and much more of it.

We will act on our sense of collective responsibility for the success of all trusts and CEOs and we will act on our moral imperative to do all we can to ensure that every child has a great education and that every community is served to the best of our collective ability. To do this we will commit to 'radical generosity'. We will be generous with our time in helping and supporting other CEOs, we will open source everything we have that works for us in the hope that it helps others too. We will engage in networks and partnerships to share best practice and resources and make connections. We will foster strong relationships with those facing the same challenges and we will do all this and more, just because it's the right thing to do, and expect nothing in return. We will pay it forward.

Having taken this enormous liberty in using the royal 'we' in formulating what I admit are some pretty bold resolutions (Do please note that research shows that people who make resolutions are ten times more likely to attain their goals than people who don't explicitly do it), the six-million-dollar question is, how do we keep them? We know it's not easy to keep our resolve as time passes and old habits of mind and action re-emerge, especially when we are faced with new challenges and problems to overcome.

Well, to help us, back to resolution number two, 'Know Your Why'. For a resolution to stick it's got to connect with something inside us, it needs to give us a sense of purpose. The difference it makes has got to be worth it. So, when we are practising self-compassion, or rediscovering our why, who and how, or being radically generous we need to understand that it will make us a better CEO, to know that it will help us serve our communities and lead our staff more effectively and to believe that we will be happier and more fulfilled as a result.

The very act of self-betterment, of taking control of how we 'Be the CEO' through these resolutions (or to be honest, any other way that means we actively determine how we are and how we behave) shouts a very big answer to the question: why?

Because we want to conduct our professional lives by design rather than by default. To be the masters of our own destiny.

Acknowledgements

Greatest of thanks to those who from the start believed in what we were doing and went to extraordinary lengths to make it happen. The early crusaders: Dean Ashton, Gary Bennell, Shane Tewes, Margaret Clarke, Lee Francis, Yateen Bhoola, and Mark Elms.

Kate Jennings, James Kenyon, Sarah Rees and Lorraine Stewart, thank you for keeping all our irons in the fire.

Roger Pryce. Your trust and support were invaluable.

Heartfelt thanks to those at the REAch2 family. Cathie Paine, Katherine Alexander and so many brilliant people in sixty great schools and a rocking central team. You inspired me to be better.

Thank you, Peter Little, for your wisdom, guidance and friendship.

Gary Bennell, so important professionally and personally. Olivia Matthews, I'll never know how you managed to make me look efficient, but you sure kept it real and made me laugh.

Richard Townsend. My first coach. Thank you.

Many thanks to the Forum Strategy team; including Michael Pain, Alice Gregson, Rachael Gacs, James Hirst, Sarah Ginns, and Lesley Pain for the opportunities I've been given and for making sense of my ramblings.

Love and thanks to the Broadstairs ladies, each and every one of you a star.